RESUME WRITING AND INTERVIEWING TECHNIQUES THAT WORK

A How-To-Do-It Manual For Librarians

Robert R. Newlen

*HOW-TO-DO-IT MANUAL
FOR LIBRARIANS*

NUMBER 148

NEAL-SCHUMAN PUBLISHERS, INC
New York   London

Published by Neal-Schuman Publishers, Inc.
100 William St., Suite 2004
New York, NY 10038

Printed and bound in the United States of America.

The paper used in this publication meets the minimum requirements of American National Standard for Information Sciences—Permanence of Paper for Printed Library Materials, ANSI Z39.48-1992. ∞

Library of Congress Cataloging-in-Publication Data

Newlen, Robert R.
  Resume writing and interviewing techniques that work: a how-to-do-it manual for librarians / Robert R. Newlen.
    p. cm.—(How-to-do-it manuals for librarians; no. 148)
  Includes bibliographical references and index.
  ISBN 1-55570-538-3 (alk. paper)
1. Library science—Vocational guidance—United States. 2. Résumés (Employment)—United States. 3. Employment interviewing—United States. I. Title. II. How-to-do-it manuals for libraries ; no. 148.
  Z682.35.V62N49 2006
    650.14—dc22
                                                                    2006005973

For Ann and Lisa, with love.

And in memoriam for Charles E. Beard.

CONTENTS

LIST OF FIGURES

FOREWORD

In *Resume Writing and Interviewing Techniques that Work: A How-To-Do-It Manual for Librarians*, Robert Newlen has revised and enhanced what I earlier called "the most important and valuable resource for anyone seeking employment in libraries today." This improved and expanded edition is excellent, and is all that any job seeker will need to be successful. The first part, "Writing a Winning Resume," offers detailed and practical tips on resume preparation through the use of worksheets designed to guide the reader in the creation of a document that is certain to capture the attention of the prospective employer. The second part, "Reviewing Successful Sample Resumes," is likely to be the most useful to some. Each chapter in this section addresses a particular category, e.g., library school student, nonsupervisory librarian, special librarian, etc., and offers sample resumes as well as specific guidelines.

The most critical stage in the employment process for the job seeker, especially one who is new to the profession, is the one in which the employer reviews resumes to select the small number of candidates to be invited to be interviewed. To be successful at this stage requires a resume which demonstrates that the applicant is one among this small number worthy of further consideration. Often well-qualified applicants are passed over at this stage because their resumes do not convey their qualifications and special abilities for the position. *Resume Writing and Interviewing Techniques that Work* offers both a process for preparing a resume that will assure qualified candidates come to the attention of prospective employers and a number of practical guidelines for helping each individual reader to apply the process to his or her particular situation.

The third part, "Interviewing Successfully," provides a detailed and complete guide to preparing for the interview and performing successfully during the interview itself. This section is likely to be especially helpful to those who have little or no experience with interviewing. Newlen includes sample questions; tips for preparing well, including how to conduct research about a prospective employer; guidance in how to handle questions about salary; and information about how to approach special types of interviews, such as screening interviews and telephone interviews.

Newlen brings considerable experience in three areas to the writing of this manual: as a manager who has hired a number of staff, as a counselor and mentor to job seekers, and as a designer and presenter of workshops on writing resumes. It is obvious that his experience as a trainer in this area is what makes this book such a valuable tool. Participants in his workshops rave about his relaxed and humorous style as well as his effectiveness in presenting the material.

The reader is guided through a series of exercises, for which worksheets are provided, to create the best possible resume. Newlen believes that an effective resume is a marketing tool and that as such it must be tailored for each position and prospective employer. His process for creating the document is designed to make it easy for the job seeker to make the necessary adjustments when preparing a special version for any position vacancy.

Resume Writing and Interviewing Techniques that Work: A How-To-Do-It Manual for Librarians will help librarians create resumes that lead to interviews. It will also benefit managers and administrators who review so many resumes. I anticipate that it will upgrade significantly the quality of resumes in the profession. This manual is essential for every librarian.

Maureen Sullivan
Organizational Development Consultant

PREFACE

Heights.
Flying.
Death.
Insects.

These are four among the ten things people in the United States fear most, according to David Wallechinsky in *The Book of Lists*. I was quite surprised to discover that resume writing and job interviewing did not make the cut. After years of experience leading workshops on this topic for fellow librarians, I cannot think of anything that seems to strike more fear in the heart of a soon-to-be employment seeker than the prospect of mastering these skills. Considering how high the stakes are—the possibility of starting a new job, advancing in a career, and launching a new life—perhaps this fear should not come as a surprise. The resume—if done correctly—can be one of the most effective ways to market yourself to employers. And interviewing well requires just as much thought and preparation as writing a resume.

I wrote *Resume Writing and Interviewing Techniques that Work: A How-To-Do-It Manual for Librarians* as an expanded and updated follow-up to an earlier work tackling the same subject. There certainly seems to be a great need for sound advice in this arena. As a workshop leader and professional who hires employees, I am constantly amazed at how casually some job seekers treat resumes—even though they are often the first introduction to employers. I have seen resumes printed on paper that was a perfect match for my Uncle Maury's pink Cadillac; resumes with grease stains (were they chowing down on chips while writing?), typos, and grammatical errors; resumes that rivaled *War and Peace* in length—you name it! Remember: A potential employer may have only 30 seconds to review a resume, so make it concise and appealing. Treat this record with the same reverence as Mom and apple pie.

After you complete the resume comes the prospect of writing a cover letter, and then, finally, preparing for interviews. A meeting with a prospective employer—if done correctly—should require the same amount of thought and preparation as writing your resume. "Winging it" rarely delivers the winning performance you need to land the job. I am always surprised to learn about the great number of job candidates—highly qualified candidates, with good references—who arrive at their interview totally unprepared.

So where do you turn for advice on writing a job-winning resume or mastering the skills to interview successfully? You don't have to look far—a whole industry has developed to exploit this anxiety. The shelves of your local bookstore and library overflow with how-to guides that practically guarantee you a job with a minimum starting salary of $ 70,000. And check out the dozens of resume services listed in the employment section of most major newspapers. These experts claim (for a small fee and your firstborn) they can design resumes that will have employers on their hands and knees, begging you to take their jobs.

What makes *Resume Writing and Interviewing Techniques that Work: A How-To-Do-It Manual for Librarians* different from all the others crowding the shelves? First, most tomes on this topic assume that one formula will work for everyone; I call these the "quick fix" resume books. They fail to recognize that every individual, as well as prospective employer, is different, and that resume writing is not one-size-fits-all. Your experience, education, accomplishments, skills, and job objectives are unique. But how do you create a resume that is tailored to your unique experience as well as the needs of your prospective employer? This handbook will guide you step by step through a series of exercises that will provide the building blocks to create a customized resume. But resume substance won't be our only concern. We will also carefully examine the *look* of the resume. Is it visually appealing? Does it jump out at your potential employer?

Most standard guides attempt to cover every job category imaginable, and if they include librarians and information professionals at all, they're usually relegated to the "other" section. I focused the basics of *Resume Writing and Interviewing Techniques that Work* specifically for our profession. You will review dozens of sample resumes from real librarians (with names and places changed to protect the innocent!). They are drawn from the full spectrum of library positions, at all career stages, and from a wide range of areas—academic, public, school, special, law, and the like. While your final resume may not resemble any of those examples exactly, it can use them as models.

While resume writing is not an easy process, you probably have all the tools you need to start writing now. Forget, the "professional" resume writer, most employers who routinely review resumes can spot these products a mile away. And you do not need costly computer programs to create a dazzling format. I created all of the resumes here using WordPerfect on my home PC. Be prepared for some hard work, though, and some tough decisions. And remember that the resume is *you*. Do you want your first impression to be marred by a typo or misspelled word? In this competitive job market, you want the best resume possible.

Once you successfully land an interview thanks to your resume, how do you prepare for it? Preparation involves conducting research about your target employer, creating sample interview questions your employer might ask, rehearsing answers for those questions, inventing questions that you will ask the interviewers, and planning your wardrobe. I look at the protocol for how to start the interview, develop your "style," examine techniques for answering interview questions, deal with salary issues, and wrap the interview up with a strong finish. While time-consuming, this preparation is guaranteed to reduce your stress level when you arrive at the face-to-face meeting. Finally, I look at post-interview tasks, such as the all-important thank-you letter.

ORGANIZATION

Resume Writing and Interviewing Techniques that Work: A How-To-Do-It Manual for Librarians is designed to simplify the process of resume writing and interviewing; its ultimate goal is to help you create a resume that will land that all-important job interview and then guide you through the interview process.

Part I, "Writing a Winning Resume," focuses on easy-to-follow steps to show you how to build a resume tailored to a job objective and to the needs of a potential employer. I emphasize creating a flexible resume, one that can be easily customized to meet changing needs.

You construct a resume through step-by-step exercises. The first step illustrates how to compile personal data and define a job objective. The next considers the substance of the resume. It describes how to define the skills needed to meet the job objective and identify personal accomplishments that support those skills. Next comes a survey of various resume formats along with guidelines to assist you in choosing the one that best showcases your individual talents and qualifications. Finally, results of all the exercises are assembled to create the final product.

Part II, "Reviewing Successful Sample Resumes," offers a look at more than two dozen samples, all based on those of "real life" librarians. They cover all areas of librarianship—public, academic, school, special, and others.

Part III, "Interviewing Successfully," focuses on how to prepare for the big day. Again, through a series of steps and checklists you become an expert job seeker guided through every aspect of the interview process. Individual chapters cover savvy advance preparation for the interview. Strategies for ways to put your best foot forward include how to research the potential employer, pose questions to the interviewer, anticipate and answer questions, and manage salary issues. Finally, post-interview tasks are discussed—thank-you letters, references, and second interviews. Special types of interview situations, such as informational, screening, and telephone interviews, are also reviewed.

The Source A section at the end of the book contains the essential file "Fill your Resume with Action Verbs."

The three indices are arranged to make pinpointing particular areas of interest easy. They are divided into general subject, job objectives and position title, and work history.

This process for writing resumes and interviewing is based on my many years of experience in giving workshops for librarians, counseling individuals on how to write resumes and prepare for interviews, and as a library manager who hires employees. Competing in today's job market is no easy task but can become more of an interesting challenge than a fearful struggle once you have the right tools. I trust you will find that this book makes the task more efficient and less stressful.

I hope *Resume Writing and Interviewing Techniques that Work: A How-To-Do-It Manual for Librarians* will help you create a polished resume and explore all the strategies necessary for successful interviewing, and that you gain the edge needed to make yourself stand out from the competition. Now, let's get to work.

ACKNOWLEDGMENTS

I'm so glad that Pat Schuman was receptive to my book pitch when I found her trying to steal a few quiet moments in a lounge chair at the pool at the Fontainebleau Hotel in Miami Beach. Since Ms. Schuman was a great inspiration to me early in my career, I'm delighted that Neal-Schuman published this book. Thanks to Charles Harmon, Michael Kelley, and all of the talented staff at Neal-Schuman for their support and encouragement of this new and expanded edition.

I remain grateful to all those friends and colleagues who shared their resumes so I could have "real life" examples. My Midwest chums were especially helpful with this expanded edition: thanks to Elinor Barrett, Melissa Carr, Erlene Bishop Killeen, Beverly Martin, and Gina Milsap. Thanks, too, to Christine Lind Hage, Joan Kaplowitz, Roberta Shaffer, Ann Symons, and Nancy Zimmerman for their expert guidance along the way. Finally, I am grateful for nearly 30 years of inspiration and support from my friend, mentor, and colleague Nancy A. Davenport.

Part I

Writing a Winning Resume

1 START THE PROCESS

Anyone who has ever put together a resume knows that it can be a lot of work. At times, you find yourself wondering whether it is really worth the effort to update old ones or, harder still, to put together new ones. When these thoughts cross your mind, remember that the initial effort you put into researching, writing, and revising your resume will reap huge benefits for you later.

This chapter will answer three basic questions about your resume:

1. What do you want your resume to do for you?
2. How can a resume help you most effectively in your job pursuit?
3. How can you both describe your personal experience and also tailor it to meet the needs of specific employers?

In the following chapters, we will first cover these and other issues in theory and then put the answers into practice. This will be done in part via a nine-step process through which you will gradually gather the information you need and then assemble it to produce a job-winning resume.

In step 1 you will create a personal history that provides an inventory of all you have done in the past, giving you a wide range of information from which to draw in later steps. This step is key, because you will make repeated reference to this information throughout the latter part of the process. Labor-intensive as it may seem, it will save you trouble down the line. In fact, it will be extremely useful at the interview stage.

OUTLINE THE TASK: WHAT IS A RESUME?

Many people think that a good resume lists every job they have ever held and cites every award they have ever won. In other words, it's like saying to a potential employer, "Let me tell you *everything* about me so I can become your employee." Remember, employers will likely be less interested in your full background than they will in the things you have done relevant to the position at hand. The first thing you do is find out what the potential employer is looking for in a candidate and ask yourself, How can I present my story so they will think I'm their ideal employee? This is why it is so critical that every decision you make about the resume be made from *the employer's perspective*. Literally get into the employer's head and think about the job from his or her perspective.

> Literally get into the employer's head and think about the job from his or her perspective.

One of the most startling things that I have discovered in my resume workshops is that many job seekers think that a single generic resume will work for all types of positions and employers. With the competition for positions now more difficult than ever, it is critical to recognize that one standard resume will not work for every employer and position. Remember, every library is different, so it is critical that every resume you submit is custom-tailored for the particular employer. Simply listing your past job responsibilities and duties will not set you apart and show you are the strongest candidate. Remember, think like the employer. Don't be overwhelmed by the prospect of having to create a custom resume for every position. The step-by-step approach in this book will help you manage this task efficiently and effectively. Keep in mind that the best resume will:

- look well designed,
- land you an interview,
- set you apart from the competition,
- market your qualifications,
- read as written in your own words,
- provide the employer with a succinct review of your accomplishments, and
- remain focused on the individual needs of the employer.

On the other hand, your resume should *never*

- recount every accomplishment,
- read like an autobiography,
- read like a formal position description,
- list every job responsibility, or
- look like an exercise in creativity.

EXAMINING THREE BASIC TYPES OF RESUMES

How do you get the right person to read your resume? We'll look at three of the most common strategies, some more effective than others. Let's explore the pros and cons of all three.

THE BLIND RESUME

Just as it shocks me that job applicants do not tailor their resumes to fit each new position, it also surprises me that many continue to send out unsolicited resumes to employers. Most seem to think that if they send out enough resumes, they are bound to be offered a job eventually. In practice, however, this is less often the case than one might think. One individual I know mailed more than 200 resumes and never received a single response. To some extent this is an indication of what is wrong with generic resumes: They simply lack the context that helps employers make basic decisions about which candidates are worth looking at more closely and which can be safely ignored.

RESUMES DESIGNED FOR A SPECIFIC OPENING

Most job seekers learn about a position from:

- an advertisement in a newspaper, professional journal, or, increasingly, a Web site;
- a vacancy announcement in an organization employment office; or
- friends, colleagues, and their "network."

Your persistence in learning as much as possible about the position and the library will make it much easier to customize or tailor your resume for the employer.

Never settle for what's described in the advertisement or vacancy announcement. Start by consulting the Web or doing a database search. Best of all, consult your professional network. You will be amazed at how small the library world can be. A colleague might refer you to another professional colleague who can provide you with the inside scoop.

Here are the kinds of questions that you want answered about your target library or employer:

- What is the overall mission of the organization?
- How does the position fit in the overall organizational structure?
- Does the library relate to a larger organizational entity, such as a university, government agency, or community structure?
- Who are the primary clients?
- What has the press reported about the organization?
- What are the challenges or problems facing the library?
- What are the library's greatest successes?

> Your persistence in learning as much as possible about the position and the library will make it much easier to customize or tailor your resume for the employer.

The data you collect about a prospective employer will help provide the edge you need to make your resume stand out from all the others scattered about the employer's desk. It will also help you tailor a job-winning cover letter, which we will discuss later.

THE "ON DEMAND" RESUME

This type of resume is one that you have ready for those unexpected situations when you need to have a resume on the spot. There are certain situations in which you want to have a resume instantly available, even though this precludes customization. For example, it is wise to have copies available when attending library conferences or other professional meetings. You never know at these events when you will be able to market yourself effectively, so always be prepared for these unplanned situations. I recall a situation early in my career when I attended a large social function for new librarians at an American Library Association conference. The event was crawling with job recruiters, and I had several opportunities to distribute my resume. You should also be aware of the fact that employers routinely share resumes with other employers. Those who recruit or hire routinely are among the best networked group I know. An employer may be impressed with your resume but decide that you aren't the best qualified candidate for a particular position. However, if the person becomes aware of other openings for which you might be qualified, he or she will often pass your resume on to those employers.

BUILDING THE RESUME WITH NINE STEP-BY-STEP EXERCISES

Let's outline the specific steps you need to take to create the job-winning resume. There are no shortcuts here, so follow each of the exercises in order. These exercises will provide you with the flexibility to try out a variety of resume formats and find the one that will best meet your individual needs. This is a time-consuming process, but most of these steps won't have to be repeated each time you create a customized resume. It's an up-front investment that will serve you well later.

These exercises will provide you with the flexibility to try out a variety of resume formats and find the one that will best meet your individual needs.

STEP 1: TAKE YOUR PERSONAL INVENTORY

This exercise provides an inventory of your life accomplishments and career. You will list all pertinent details related to your job history, education, volunteer and professional activities, publications, and so forth.

STEP 2: DEFINE YOUR JOB OBJECTIVE

Defining your job objective is key to successful resume writing. Should you always identify an objective on your resume? How will the employer interpret this information? Can it ever be used to your disadvantage? We will answer each of these questions and assess how you should best use the job objective statement.

STEP 3: DESCRIBE THE SKILLS OR QUALITIES NEEDED TO MEET YOUR JOB OBJECTIVE

Having defined the job objective, what qualities can you define that are most important for achieving it? You will identify the top skills needed and evaluate each one using your knowledge of the employer.

STEP 4: IDENTIFY ACCOMPLISHMENTS AND ABILITIES THAT SUPPORT EACH SKILL

With this step, you will carefully review your personal inventory and write supporting statements about each skill. We will examine action verbs and those techniques for succinctly communicating your strongest abilities and skills.

STEP 5: WRITE THE SUMMARY OR HIGHLIGHTS OF QUALIFICATIONS

In this exercise, you will identify the top four or five qualifications that demonstrate why you are the best candidate for the job.

STEP 6: CHOOSE THE BEST RESUME FORMAT

Choosing the best resume format is essential for marketing yourself and attracting the attention of your potential employer. We will examine three different formats. The first and most common is chronological, which is a listing of your positions in reverse chronological order. Functional is the next format, which highlights your strongest skill or quality categories. The last format, which is often overlooked by many resume writers, is the combination format, which contains elements of the first two formats. We will assess the strengths and weaknesses of each format vis-à-vis your career and resume needs.

> Choosing the best resume format is essential for marketing yourself and attracting the attention of your potential employer.

STEP 7: ASSEMBLE THE RESUME

This is where we pull all the elements together and actually write the resume. We'll look at suggested headings for each category and decide what and how much information should be included.

STEP 8: REVIEW HOW IT LOOKS

This is one of the most important steps we will consider. Once the content of the resume is complete, we'll evaluate its "look" to make sure it is visually appealing and attractive. We will also consider length, formats, allowing for plenty of white space, tips on using graphics, and how to select appropriate paper that will make your resume stand out.

STEP 9: CONDUCT A FINAL CHECKLIST

Once we have completed the exercises, we'll do a final review to make sure your final checklist is in perfect shape. This checklist, which includes areas most often overlooked by resume writers, will come in handy every time you update your resume.

Now, let's tackle that first exercise!

STEP 1: CREATING HISTORY WORKSHEETS TO TAKE A PERSONAL INVENTORY

Taking time to compile a personal inventory of your life is an important step before actually beginning to write the resume. Don't panic! I promise you won't have to analyze your relationship with your mother. The personal inventory serves two key purposes. First, it's an excellent source to refer back to as you customize your resume to specific job objectives and employers. Second, by reviewing the inventory before an interview, you can refresh your memory about your skills and accomplishments. You are going to look at each of the following areas in detail, using the worksheet with each of these categories that is included at the end of the chapter:

- professional work history
- nonprofessional work history
- education, specialized training, and language skills
- professional association involvement
- publications or Web sites
- presentations

- research and grant activities
- volunteer work and personal interests

Obviously, all of the data you gather won't be included, but it's important to get an overall picture so that you have all the building blocks ready with which to assemble a job-winning resume. When your job objective changes or you inevitably need to update the resume, having this inventory ready will save you the trouble of reinventing the wheel. Bear in mind that certain personal information is not appropriate to include in your resume (see Figure 2-6).

Now, let's review what should be included under each personal history category.

PROFESSIONAL WORK HISTORY

Start by listing *all* position titles and organizations for which you have worked, including dates of employment. It is generally sufficient just to include the years in the position (e.g., 2000 to present) and omit specific months. Remember to review your entire career; not all of your positions may necessarily appear on your resume, but you don't want to leave anything unexamined. Include a description of your accomplishments in this position. This is best achieved by doing it with "bulleted" one-line descriptions. It is essential these one-liners be in your own words and *not* lifted from a formal job description or a laundry list of your duties. Here are some good questions to consider in describing each of your positions:

What are the major responsibilities?

How many employees have you supervised?

Is it possible to quantify your accomplishments?

- If you manage staff, what number of people have you supervised?
- If you administer a budget, what is the amount?
- If circulation improved, by how much and over what period?

What personal skills have you developed?

- When have you worked well independently?
- When have you worked well as a member of a team?
- Do you work under minimal supervision? Have you worked successfully under pressure or deadlines?

Did you initiate or implement a new program or procedure?

Did you display leadership qualities, even if you weren't in a formal management position?

- What leadership skills have you acquired?
- Have you chaired a committee or task force or headed a special project?
- What have you accomplished outside of your required responsibilities or job description?

If you served on a team or task force, what was the outcome of your work?

- If recommendations were made, were they actually implemented?
- How did your work improve the performance of the library?
- What were the positive results?

Have you won any awards?
What problems have you solved?

- How did you find solutions?

What writing skills have you developed?

- Have you prepared reports?
- Have you written performance appraisals?
- Have you participated in any grant writing?

Have you done any public speaking or made presentations?

- Have you presented before professional groups?
- Have you presented at a state or national conference?

What are your technology skills?

- Have you been involved in writing requirements, selecting vendors, or working with user groups?
- What systems do you know?
- Where do you have the greatest proficiencies?

> Remember to review your entire career; not all of your positions may necessarily appear on your resume, but you don't want to leave anything unexamined.

Accounting for periods of unemployment is especially important. Resume writers often forget to mention periods of unemployment due to child care, full-time academic pursuits, and the like, but any significant gap in employment is a red flag for the potential employer, who will assume the worst —incarceration, undercover spy, or political terrorist, at the very least. While it is not necessary to indicate why you left a position in a resume, *always* be truthful if this issue is raised in an interview situation. We will consider this in more detail in the chapters on interviewing.

Finally, don't neglect to include any consulting or freelance work. Have you done private research? Indexed a book? Prepared bibliographies for publications? These are all important skills, and you don't want to omit them from your resume.

NONPROFESSIONAL WORK HISTORY

Why on earth would you want to mention a former job delivering pizzas? Or waiting tables? Or working as a clerk in retail? Some job candidates shoot themselves in the foot by not revealing what they consider to be nonprofessional work experience because they fear they won't be taken seriously. Of course, including nonprofessional work experience on a resume is not appropriate for everyone, but for some job seekers, such as those just out of library school, these jobs can be part of your marketing strategy.

Waiter/waitress, receptionist, telephone solicitor, or camp counselor—all of these positions may actually have some relevance to the job you are seeking. Take the waiter/waitress position, for example. It requires juggling multiple demands and interacting with a wide range of people; can you think of any better preparation for coping with the demands of the reference desk?

For a position involving extensive telephone reference, I once interviewed a candidate who mentioned in passing that she had worked as a telephone reservation clerk with a major motel chain. This information was omitted from her resume, but what better experience for telephone reference? I hired her on the spot!

EDUCATION, SPECIALIZED TRAINING, AND LANGUAGE SKILLS

Make a complete list of the following:

What schools have you attended? What were the dates of enrollment? What degrees do you hold?

Did you receive awards, scholarships, fellowships, internships, professional recognition, honorary societies, or superior grade point average?

Did you participate in drama or debate?

Did you take any training courses? What were the dates of completion? What skills were acquired?

Did you take any technology-related courses?

> Some job candidates shoot themselves in the foot by not revealing what they consider to be nonprofessional work experience because they fear they won't be taken seriously.

What is your degree of proficiency with databases, software, Web-related technologies, hardware, and networks?

Remember: There are hardly any positions in libraries today that don't require at least some technology-related skills. When it comes time to write the resume, remember to include only those courses and skills that are directly relevant to the position you are seeking.

Have you lived in a foreign country?

What are your language abilities?

What are your skill levels in each language? Can you read or converse fluently?

PROFESSIONAL ASSOCIATION INVOLVEMENT

Many job applicants overlook this important area which can really set you apart from the competition. While some resume writers list memberships in professional organizations, they frequently forget to indicate their level of involvement. A prospective employer is interested in learning about your level of participation in these associations because it demonstrates initiative and commitment to the profession.

As with other types of volunteer work, you have probably gained valuable experience through professional association involvement that has direct relevance to the position you seek. If you don't have the opportunity to chair meetings in your current job, then don't forget to mention that you chaired a committee in a special library association, a library school association, or local library association. Or perhaps your prospective job requires budgetary experience and you have no related duties in your current position. Then describe your position as treasurer of a regional library association. Documenting participation in a professional association can make an instant connection with a prospective employer who may be active in the same organization or who may have held the same position in another organization and thus understands the complexity and responsibility involved.

For library school students or recent graduates, be sure to list memberships even if you haven't had an opportunity yet to become active in the respective professional association. Be sure to list attendance at any association or professional conference.

PUBLICATIONS OR WEB SITES

List all articles, papers, or books you have written. Be sure to include any experience in writing for association or staff newsletters. This can include writing you have done in any volunteer capacity. Also, be sure to document any writing or design you

> Documenting participation in a professional association can make an instant connection with a prospective employer who may be active in the same organization.

have done for Web sites or Web publications. Keep a master file of these publications so you can quickly make copies when writing samples are required for applications or interviews. I will discuss more about this in the section on interviewing.

PRESENTATIONS

List any presentations you have given at professional conferences, workshops, or seminars. Be sure to include the dates of these presentations. Also, include any courses you have taught or tours you have led. Be sure to include presentations to groups which you may give in your current position and describe your role. Do you make presentations to managers or decision makers? Do you prepare PowerPoint presentations? If so, be sure to state this. What is your role in the presentation? Be sure to quantify and indicate the size of the audience.

RESEARCH AND GRANT ACTIVITIES

List any ongoing research. Have you received grants to support your research or written grant proposals in the workplace? Don't neglect to mention these items. They are especially important for those applying for academic positions.

VOLUNTEER WORK AND PERSONAL INTERESTS

Like involvement in professional organizations, experience gained on your own time is often neglected by resume writers. Remember, just because you weren't paid doesn't mean this experience wasn't worthwhile. Documenting volunteer work is important for several reasons. Today, many employers look for well-rounded individuals, people with a healthy balance of professional and personal life.

Following is a list of transferable skills and leadership qualities of volunteer work:

- organizational skills
- public speaking
- fund-raising
- grant writing
- budgeting
- publicity
- meeting deadlines
- coordinating meetings
- event planning
- leading a team
- recruitment

- training
- scheduling

Think about other skills you have gained in your community groups. Let's face it, if you can successfully manage a group of children as a room mother/father in an elementary school, you can probably handle the many pressures of library work! Be sure to mention how long you have been involved in these activities. To describe volunteer work positions, use the same process as described for professional positions.

List your personal interests and sports activities. Again, including these may not always be appropriate (skydiving, bungee jumping, sword swallowing, and nude modeling are probably best omitted), but they can often make an important connection with a potential employer.

REVIEWING THE SAMPLE RESUME OF JANET TAYLOR

To illustrate how a personal history worksheet is developed, we will use Janet Taylor as an example here and in subsequent exercises so that you can follow the complete development of a resume step by step.

Janet is the assistant director of a medium-size public library district, and she is seeking the next logical step in her career: a position as a director in a smaller library system. She has solid skills and qualifications necessary for this type of position and is now faced with the challenge of marketing her strengths via her resume. Our first step will be to examine the resume Janet wrote before she completed the nine-step process in this manual (see Figure 1-1).

Figure 1-1   Sample "Before" Resume of Janet Taylor

```
                        Resume of
                        Janet F. Taylor
                        27 Chelsea Court
                        Woodland Springs, AR   72764
                        501-770-2828


                        Relevant Experience

Jan., 2001 -  Assistant Director, Redford County Public Library
              District

              Serves on the newly created Library Building Committee.
              Worked extensivly on implementing plans/services for
              this new building. Created the Library's Disaster Plan,
              ADA Strategic Plan, In-Charge Manual, and Supervisor
              Management Documents.  Aides Department Heads in creat-
              ing job descriptions and solving personal problems.
              Worked with the Maintenance Dept. to make their transi-
              tion to the new building easier.


2000          Acting Director, Redford County Public Library District

              (Jan.-June 2000) Negotiated the new building plans
              through the political obstacles of Redford County
              Public Library District. Submitted the first budget
              ever that was passed on the first try by the Trustees.
              Learned to balance Staff, Trustee, and Community needs.


Feb., 1999-   Associate Librarian/Head of Technical Services
Jan., 2000    (Redford County Public Library District)

              Worked actively on the new building referendum with
              Staff, Trustees, and community groups. Learned to manage
              a multi-faceted department.


1998-1989     Associate Librarian/Head of Reference
              (Redford County Public Library District)

              Worked with my Department to form a service-oriented
              team and a more in-depth collection. Was responsible
              for the Library's building renovation in 1998
```

(continued)

Figure 1-1 Sample "Before" Resume of Janet Taylor (*Continued*)

<u>Other Experience</u>

Reference Librarian (1994-1997), and Elementary School Librarian (1992-1994). A variety of part-time positions between 1990 and 1992 include Substitute Refrence Librarian at Springdale College, Documents Technician at University of Arkansas Undergraduate Library.

<u>Education</u>

1987-1990   Grinnell College, Grinnell, IA (B.A.)
             Major: Sociology   Minor: Italian
             Member: Debate Team
                      Student Council
                      Choral Choir

1992-1994   University of North Texas School of Library Science (M.S.)
Member: Library School Student Assoc.

<u>Membership and Committees</u>

American Library Association
Arkansas Library Association
Staff Develoment Comm.

<u>Publications</u>

2002   "First Line Supervisors: On the Edge", LAMA Journal, Fall, 2002.

<u>Other</u>

Good health. Divorced with two children.

Take a moment and think of yourself as the employer who will be the selecting official for a public library director position. Assuming you have plenty of time on your hands, a careful read of Janet's resume might reveal some of the qualities needed for her target position. But remember, the average resume reader will spend less than *30 seconds* with Janet's resume, so her qualifications must virtually jump off the page and grab the reader's attention. Spend a few minutes reviewing the resume and jot down your concerns. Here are some of the major weaknesses:

- There is no job objective, which is odd, considering that she has a stated objective.
- There is no summary of qualifications to demonstrate why she is the best choice for this position.
- The overall format is visually unappealing. The dates of her employment have too much emphasis.
- There are many typos—the kiss of death!
- Acronyms appear that may have no meaning to the prospective employer.
- Janet's accomplishments under each job read more like job descriptions or official position descriptions.
- She has not elaborated on the extent of her involvement in the professional associations listed.
- She has included inappropriate personal information.
- She has missed opportunities to quantify her accomplishments.

ASSESSING JANET'S PERSONAL HISTORY

Now, let's follow Janet step by step as she completes her personal history worksheet. As you will see, Janet omitted a great deal of significant information that will be useful in demonstrating that she is highly qualified for a director's position. At this stage, she remembers that this is not the time to be selective. Her goal is to get everything down and edit later.

PROFESSIONAL WORK HISTORY

Let's look at Janet's complete work history. She uses bulleted one-line statements to describe her positions.

Assistant Director, Redford County Public Library District, Redford, AR
2001 to present

- Assisted director in managing a budget of $4.5 million, a staff of 105, and a collection of over 275,000 items
- Worked closely with board consisting of seven members
- Library Building Committee—chaired this committee for two years
- Coordinated transition team to plan move to new building
- Designed library's disaster plan
- Designed and implemented ADA strategic plan
- Wrote supervisory manual for the library
- Advised five department heads on writing job descriptions
- Counseled department heads on employee problems

Acting Director, Redford County Public Library District
2000

- For six-month period, served as acting director
- Negotiated the new building plans with board and county government
- Worked closely with community groups on all aspects of building plan
- Proposed budget that was passed on the first attempt by library board
- Responsible for all administrative functions of the library

Associate Librarian/Head of Technical Services, Redford County Public Library District
1999–2000

- Managed all aspects of technical service department, including acquisitions, serials, interlibrary loan, and cataloging functions
- Extensive use of OCLC and the Dynix automated library system
- Experience with AACR2 and MARC formats
- Extensive audiovisual cataloging
- Supervised a staff of seven
- Outstanding performance evaluation

Head of Reference, Redford County Public Library District
1998–99

- Supervised a staff of 8 reference librarians and 4 library aides
- Served on the collection development committee
- Chaired committee on user access
- Revised and improved library reference guide
- Developed and monitored database budget of over $25,000

Reference Librarian, San Angelo Free Public Library, San Angelo, TX
1994–97

- Provided extensive reference service
- Coordinated staff training on new online catalog
- Redesigned quick reference collection for more efficient use

Elementary School Librarian, Sam Houston Elementary School, Eagle Pass, TX
1992–94

- Developed and maintained library and multimedia center for school of 350 students
- Created parent advisory committee for library to increase parent volunteers
- Implemented automated circulation control for the library

Substitute Reference Assistant, Springdale College, Springdale, TX
1990–92

- Performed part-time reference services for college library serving 800 students
- Staffed reference and circulation desk
- Routinely used college's automated catalog to assist patrons

Documents Technician (part-time), Grinnell College Undergraduate Library, Grinnell, IA
1988–90

- Worked with federal depository library collection

- Sorted and shelved documents
- Maintained collection

NONPROFESSIONAL WORK HISTORY
Admissions Office Clerk, Grinnell College, 1988–89

- Processed applications, entering tracking information in computer system
- Responded to telephone and letter inquiries from prospective students

EDUCATION, SPECIALIZED TRAINING, AND LANGUAGE SKILLS
B.A., 1990, Grinnell College, Grinnell, IA. Major in Sociology. Minor in Italian.

- Debate team member, 1987–90
- Member, student council
- Member, choral choir

M.S. in Library Science, 1994, University of North Texas School of Library Science, Denton, TX.

- Programs committee, library science student association
- Served on team that coordinated quarterly programs for students

PROFESSIONAL ASSOCIATION INVOLVEMENT
While Janet's current resume reflects the breadth of her professional involvement, it doesn't reflect the extent of her activity.

American Library Association, 1993 to present

Member, Supervisory Skills Committee, Personnel Administration Section, Library Administration and Management Association, 2001 to present. Served on the subcommittee that implemented a listserv on supervisory skills. Helped to plan and implement 2002 program at annual conference, "First Line Supervisors: On the Edge."

Arkansas Library Association, 1989 to present

Secretary, 1989–90. Took minutes of all meetings. Member, 50th anniversary Committee. Served on team that planned and implemented association events for celebration. This included a Tribute Day event involving Arkansas legislators and media.

PUBLICATIONS OR WEB SITES

Coedited article on program presented at annual conference, American Library Association: "First Line Supervisors: On the Edge," *Library Administration and Management Journal*, Fall, 2002.

VOLUNTEER WORK AND PERSONAL INTERESTS

Served for two years as a volunteer for Reading is Fun program tutoring elementary school students on weekends (2000–01).

Through St. Mary Parish, coordinated volunteer visits to three nursing and long-term care facilities in Redford, AR (2002).

Personal interests: Embroidery, rollerblading, travel, French language group

This is quite an inventory! You can see that when Janet started to analyze her background, she recalled a great deal of information that will be useful in her revised resume. This is the primary purpose of the inventory—to get the big picture so that you can pick and choose what is most relevant to your targeted position and employer. Now it's your turn! Use the following pages (Figure 1-2 through 1-7) to create your own personal inventory or create one on your PC or in a notebook. The personal history is hard work, but it will pay off when you move on to the next steps to develop resume content. Again, you will be referring back to this inventory throughout the building process. When you finally land that interview, your personal inventory will be an excellent document to review to refresh yourself on your accomplishments. So let's make the most of this inventory.

> When you finally land that interview, your personal inventory will be an excellent document to review to refresh yourself on your accomplishments.

Figure 1-2   Worksheet: Professional Work Experience

1. List every position of any professional job you have held.
Remember:
√ Include every job, even if you don't think you will include it in your final resume.
√ Account for periods of unemployment.
√ Include consulting or freelance work.

_____

_____

_____

_____

_____

_____

_____

_____

_____

_____

_____

2. Write a "bulleted" list of your accomplishments for every job.
√ This is a brainstorming assignment. Write in your own voice.

_____

_____

_____

_____

_____

_____

_____

_____

_____

_____

_____

_____

Figure 1-3 Worksheet: Nonprofessional Work Experience

This exercise is especially important for recent library school graduates or those just entering the profession.

1. List every nonprofessional position you have held.
√ Include every position—even if you don't think you will include it in your final resume.
√ Address any skills, such as communication and leadership, that these positions might highlight.

_____

_____

_____

_____

_____

_____

_____

_____

_____

_____

_____

_____

_____

_____

_____

_____

_____

_____

_____

_____

_____

_____

_____

_____

Figure 1-4 Worksheet: Education, Specialized Training, and Language Skills

1. List any awards, scholarships, fellowships, and/or internships you have received.

_____

_____

_____

_____

_____

_____

_____

_____

_____

_____

_____

_____

_____

_____

2. Describe your educational history in detail, paying special attention to any educational honors or other notable successes. Be alert to coursework related to technology.

_____

_____

_____

_____

_____

_____

_____

_____

_____

_____

_____

_____

_____

_____

_____

_____

Figure 1-5   Worksheet: Professional Association Involvement

1. List any professional organizations with which you are involved and describe your level of involvement with each.

Remember:

√ Discuss any skills you have acquired.

√ Include any leadership positions you have held.

_____

_____

_____

_____

_____

_____

_____

_____

_____

_____

_____

_____

2. List any recent professional conferences you have attended and describe your role in each.

Remember:

√ List any panels or committees on which you served.

_____

_____

_____

_____

_____

_____

_____

_____

_____

_____

_____

Figure 1-6 Worksheet: Publications, Presentations, Research, and Grant Activities

1. List any articles, essays or books you have published.
√ Include any writing you have done for association and staff newsletters and publications.
√ If you maintain or regularly contribute to a blog, consider mentioning this as well.

_____

_____

_____

_____

_____

_____

_____

2. List any talks or presentations you have given.
√ Mention any speeches given at professional conferences or while consulting, even if this leads to some overlap with other worksheets.

_____

_____

_____

_____

_____

_____

_____

3. List any professional or academic research you have performed and describe any grants you have received.
√ Include both ongoing and past activities.

_____

_____

_____

_____

_____

_____

Figure 1-7   Worksheet: Volunteer Work and Personal Interests

1. List all volunteer work you have done.
√ Remember to focus on the skills you acquired that could be transferable to paying positions.

_____

_____

_____

_____

_____

_____

_____

_____

_____

_____

2. List all personal and sport activities.
√ Remember these can make an instant connection with employers.

_____

_____

_____

_____

_____

_____

_____

_____

_____

_____

_____

_____

2 ASSEMBLE THE RIGHT STUFF

As we review each of these areas in exercises, we'll continue to use Janet Taylor as an example. Your personal worksheet for each of these exercises is included at the end of this chapter.

STEP 2: DESCRIBING THE JOB OBJECTIVE

Before you begin to write your resume, it is crucial that you develop a fully expressed description of the job, position, or post for which you plan to apply. This explanation is an important part in the development of a truly successful resume, as it will help keep you consistent and on track. Whenever you find yourself in doubt about whether an item should be included, think about it in terms of your job objective. Only those things that support the objective should be included. Those things that do not fit but seem necessary must be tailored to fit your goal. If you take this process of comparison seriously, your resume will be focused, appropriate, and compelling, demonstrating your strengths to potential employers without dwelling on irrelevant details. The job objective is not, as some experts argue, "wasted real estate" on the resume. Instead it is a powerful means to sharpen and amplify the information that follows it.

There are two possible forms that the job objective can take depending on whether you are applying for a specific position or

> The job objective is not, as some experts argue, "wasted real estate" on the resume. Instead it is a powerful means to sharpen and amplify the information that follows it.

a more general type of position for which there may be a variety of potential employers. The first is fairly straightforward, as you should have a clear sense of the actual title of the post. Examples of these of job objectives include:

- Media Specialist, Parkwood Middle School
- Young Adult Librarian, Greene County Public Library
- Branch Librarian, Kenton County Public Library
- Director, Santa Cruz Public Library
- Acquisitions Librarian, Ohio State Library
- Web Designer, Allen County Public Library
- Young Adult Librarian, Rogers Public Library

Including the job title at the top of the resume as your objective tends to have a positive effect. Among other things, it indicates to the reader that you are sufficiently interested in the position to have modified your resume.

The second, more general, type of job objective is more difficult to write. If it is phrased too broadly, it will likely be uninformative for potential employers and not particularly useful to you in the composition of your resume. If, on the other hand, it is too specific, it may keep employers from considering you for jobs for which you might otherwise be qualified. Here are some examples of this second type of job objective:

- Electronic resources librarian in a college or university
- Public services librarian with a specialization in instruction
- Archivist/special collections librarian
- Entry-level reference position in a public library
- Corporate librarian
- Reference librarian with specialty in information literacy
- Head of technical services in a public library system
- School library media specialist
- Systems administrator with specialty in portals
- Collection development librarian

LEARNING HOW TO DETERMINE YOUR JOB OBJECTIVE

If you do not have a clear sense of your job objective, you can start by thinking through these questions:

- What do you want to do next?
- What type of library or organization do you want to do it in?
- At what level would you like to start—entry, supervisory, or managerial?

If you need some help, two of my favorite books for career planning and skill assessment are *The Librarian's Career Guidebook*, Priscilla K. Shontz, editor (Lanham, MD: Scarecrow Press, 2004, ISBN 0-8108-5034-6) and *Jump Start Your Career in Library and Information Science* by Priscilla K. Shontz (Lanham, MD: Scarecrow Press, 2002, ISBN 0-8108-4084-7).

Once you have clear answers to each of these three questions, try to connect and narrow your response to form an actual statement of what you hope to do. Try to make your final job objective as precise as possible—under no circumstances should it be a generic statement. Some job objective statements to avoid include:

- A challenging position as a librarian that takes advantage of my education
- Position as an entry-level cataloger with career-enhancing opportunities
- Library management position that will utilize my can do attitude
- Position as young adult librarian with a rapid promotion ladder
- Entry-level reference position with outstanding training opportunities

Most of these statements reveal the applicant's expectations, not the employer's. By way of example, let's take a look at Janet Taylor's job objective statement, which is fairly straightforward. First, here are her answers to the questions listed above:

Q: What do you want to do next?
A: Work in a position with greater supervisory and administrative responsibility.

Q: What type of library or organization do you want to do it in?
A: A small or medium-size public library.

Q: At what level?
A: As a director.

With these questions answered, Janet's statement reads as follows:

Objective: Position as a director in a small or medium-size public library.

> Try to make your final job objective as precise as possible—under no circumstances should it be a generic statement.

STEP 3: DEFINING THE SKILLS AND QUALITIES NEEDED TO MEET YOUR JOB OBJECTIVE

Once your job objective has been determined, the next step is to put it to use by identifying the skills and qualities that will best support it. This can be difficult, but you can make it easier for yourself if you stop thinking like an applicant and try to think like a potential employer. If your objective is a specific job at a particular institution, the easiest way to go about doing this is to carefully read and reflect on the job announcement, paying special attention to any traits or abilities that it identifies directly. On the other hand, if your objective is more general, you may still need to think about the issue creatively.

Sometimes it helps to imagine that you are looking to hire someone with your job objective. How could you start to decide the skills he or she would need to have? Try this experiment:

- Review every aspect of the job position.
- Brainstorm the skills needed to be most successful in this position.
- Write them down in a list.
- Prioritize the list.
- Narrow the list down to four or five of the most important qualities or skills.

MATCHING OBJECTIVES WITH SKILLS AND ABILITIES

Let's look at some job objectives and the most important skills or qualities needed to be successful in that position. Remember, concentrate on what the employer considers most beneficial.

Job objective: Acquisitions department head in an academic library

1. Financial and accounting skills
2. Electronic acquisitions experience
3. Supervisory experience
4. Coordinating acquisition procedures

> Stop thinking like an applicant and try to think like a potential employer.

Job objective: Reference librarian specializing in health sciences

1. Reference skills
2. Background in health sciences
3. Oral communication skills
4. Expertise in searching health-related electronic resources

Job objective: Systems/Access Services librarian

1. Experience with a broad range of library technologies
2. Knowledge of electronic information resources and tools, and Web-based technologies
3. Familiarity with information literacy principles

Job objective: Head of children's services in a public library system

1. Ability to plan and direct children's/young adult collections
2. Supervisory experience
3. Knowledge of children's/young adult resources
4. Oral communication skills

Job objective: State Librarian of Vermont

1. Knowledgeable about library technology
2. Ability to manage a complex organization
3. Background in public finance and human resource management
4. Experience in governmental processes at all levels—local, state, and federal

Job objective: Metadata services cataloger

1. Knowledge of cataloging principles and standards
2. Experience in creating and utilizing metadata
3. Experience with institutional depository program software

Job objective: Instructional Service librarian

1. Experience in providing library instruction and reference
2. Knowledge of electronic resources

3. Knowledge of or experience with instructional management systems or development of online tutorials
4. Writing skills

First, Janet does some brainstorming on the critical skills and
qualities needed for this position:

Experience in a public library system
Fiscal management skills
Supervisory experience
Oral and communication skills
Ability to interact with community, library boards, and local
   governments
Leadership skills
Experience with technology
Organizational skills
Strategic planning

She then narrows the list to the following:

Supervisory and administrative skills
Community and governmental relations experience
Technology planning skills
Fiscal management skills

STEP 4: IDENTIFYING ACCOMPLISHMENTS AND ABILITIES THAT SUPPORT EACH SKILL OR QUALITY

Having identified the most important skills and qualities needed
to meet your job objective, it's now time to write supporting statements for each one. In other words, prove that you have the experience to do the job! Start by reviewing your personal
inventory—your hard work on this earlier exercise is now going
to pay off.

For each skill or quality, you are going to write several one-
line supporting statements. Carefully analyze the experience you
have acquired that is directly relevant to each one.

EMPLOYING TOP TEN TIPS

Here are some essential tips for writing those one-liners:

1. Keep the language tight and phrase short.
2. Don't use the first person "I."
3. Use incomplete sentences like:
   planned and implemented the network
   initiated after-school reading hour
   coordinated acquisition policies
   evaluated network proposals
   established cataloging policies
   wrote user instruction training manual
   administered budget of over $ 30 million
   simplified archival acquisition procedures

4. Use action verbs such as: achieved, administered, compiled, converted, effected, expanded, improved, increased, planned, reorganized, streamlined, and trained. A comprehensive list of action verbs is included in Source A.

5. Avoid passive terms found in formal job descriptions such as:
   Responsible for . . .
   In charge of . . .
   Duties included . . .
   Scope of responsibilities included . . .

6. Use plain English and avoid "insider" terminology and acronyms that may have no meaning to the resume reader. Remember that the potential employer may not be a librarian and may have only limited or no knowledge of the field. Be specific and don't use undefined acronyms or vague phrases like:
   Facilitated in-service computerized circulation
   Represented the library on District Steering Team for WPL-WASB Pilot Project
   Determined community needs and services
   Represented the section on interlibrary teams

7. Think about writing these one-liners in terms of your accomplishments. This is what will sell you to the prospective employer. Whenever possible, *quantify* your skills and illustrate results. Demonstrate to your potential employer that you are action and result oriented:
   How many people did you supervise?

How much money did you save?
What size budget did you manage?
How much did circulation increase?
How did productivity increase?
What did you produce?
How many students did you train?
What were the results of the programs you implemented?
How much time did you save?

Figure 2-1   Turning Weak Statements into Strong Statements

The following are weak statements followed by stronger revised ones:

Weak: "Significantly boosted circulation in my library."
Strong: "Increased circulation by 20,000 titles in two years."

Weak: "Looked at library software and hardware."
Strong: "Evaluated and recommended an automated circulation system, which was selected."

Weak: "Created bibliographies on several subjects."
Strong: "Wrote bibliographies on current national defense and foreign affairs topics on a continuing basis."

Weak: "Supported the technical services section."
Strong: "Participated on team that accessed new materials and prepared materials for cataloging."

Weak: "Changed procedures for checking-in serials."
Strong: "Successfully streamlined procedures for serial check-in, which saved eight hours of staff time a week."

8. When you have worked with a team—say so! If you co-authored a report, be sure to indicate it.

9. Don't be modest. However, be wary of using too many superlatives; while you may be "the most productive" or "the most innovative," it's better to demonstrate how and why you are productive or innovative.

10. Don't exaggerate or, worse, lie. Never include anything you wouldn't want printed on the front page of the *New York Times*.

To achieve her goal of a position as director of a public library, Janet identified the following skills and qualities:

Supervisory and administrative skills
Community and government relations experience
Technology skills
Fiscal management skills

Using her personal inventory, the following are one-liners that Janet wrote for each:
Supervisory and administrative skills

- *Wrote comprehensive library disaster plan*
- *Assisted in administration of a staff of over 100*
- *Coordinated transition team to move central library to a new building*
- *Chaired library building committee and submitted plan that was approved by library board*
- *Wrote supervisory manual for the library*
- *Counseled department heads on employee problems*

Technology skills

- *Evaluated library systems and made recommendations that were accepted*
- *Helped to implement installation of new Dynix system*

Community and government relations

- *Designed and implemented ADA Strategic Plan*
- *Met monthly with library board*
- *Represented library on Redford County Business Development Committee*
- *Negotiated building plans*

Fiscal management skills

- *Assisted in managing a budget of $4.5 million*
- *Cochaired audit review committee*
- *Proposed a budget (1994) that was passed on the first attempt by the library board*

STEP 5: WRITING THE SUMMARY OR HIGHLIGHTS OF QUALIFICATIONS

Not to be indelicate, but the summary of qualifications is where you grab the potential employer by the throat, saying, Don't pass over this resume, because I've got what it takes to do your job! The summary of qualifications is your opportunity to self-market. Since these highlights appear just below the job objective, this is one of the first resume elements that the reader will see. Once again, you need to think like the employer.

To help you write the qualifications, review step 4 and match your most outstanding accomplishments—four or five statements are best—with the skills you perceive to be most important to the employer. This is no time to be modest! Be brief and to the point, and highlight your strongest qualifications as they relate to the job objective. If a statement does not specifically reinforce the job objective, eliminate it. Every qualification must be focused on your objective.

Here are some examples of job objectives with a summary of qualifications.

Job objective: Reference librarian specializing in health sciences

Summary of qualifications:

- Three years' experience working in reference in major medical school library.
- Expert searching experience with a wide range of health databases, including Ovid and NLM.
- Developed innovative training and instructional manuals in print and electronic formats.
- Strong educational background in health sciences.

Job objective: Supervisory government documents librarian

Summary of qualifications:

- In-depth experience in working with a federal depository collection.
- Extensive background in cataloging government documents and maps.
- Supervised a staff of seven.
- Ability to work well in fast-paced, high-pressure environment.

Job objective: Interlibrary loan librarian

Summary of qualifications:

- Strong skills in working with integrated library computer systems.
- Excellent knowledge of copyright law.
- Broad knowledge of document delivery systems and networks.
- Two years' experience in electronic document delivery.

Job objective: Associate Professor of library and information science

Summary of qualifications:

- Graduate teaching experience at large university.
- ABD in Library Science.
- Extensive experience in information retrieval systems and services.
- Recognized for innovative teaching technologies.

Job objective: Head of children's services in public library system

Summary of qualifications:

- In-depth knowledge of children's literature and services.
- Five years' experience as branch librarian with specialization in service to children/young adults.
- Extensive supervisory experience.
- Developed award-winning reading programs for children.

After carefully checking to see if each qualification supported the job objective, Janet chose the following:

Job objective: Position as director in a small or medium-size public library

Summary of qualifications:

- Outstanding supervisory and administrative skills gained in dynamic, medium-size public library.
- Extensive experience in evaluation and implementation of a broad range of library technologies.
- Assisted in managing a budget of over $4 million.
- Proven skills in government and community relations.

USING WORKSHEETS TO WRITE YOUR OWN SUMMARY

Fill in the worksheets in Figures 2-2 through 2-5, which will assist you in completing the steps outlined in this chapter. Figure 2-6 will provide tips on what you should *not* include. When you are finished, turn to the next chapter, on choosing a resume format.

Figure 2-2   Identify Your Job Objective

√ Make your objective brief, clear, and to the point.
√ Distinguish your job objective from your job expectations.
√ Do not describe your career.

_____

_____

_____

_____

_____

_____

Figure 2-3   Define the Skills and Qualities Needed to Meet Your Job Objective

√ Are you thinking from potential employers' points of view?
√ What might be their expectations?
√ Which skills do you think they are looking for?
√ What qualities do you think they would value?

_____

_____

_____

_____

_____

_____

_____

_____

_____

_____

_____

_____

_____

_____

_____

_____

_____

_____

_____

_____

_____

_____

_____

_____

Figure 2-4   Identify Accomplishments and Abilities that Support Each Skill or Quality

√ Write several one-line supporting statements for each.
√ Lead with action verbs—see Source A.
√ Quantify in specifics whenever possible.

1. What are your accomplishments?

_____

_____

_____

_____

_____

_____

_____

_____

_____

_____

_____

_____

2. What are your abilities?

_____

_____

_____

_____

_____

_____

_____

_____

_____

_____

_____

Figure 2-5   Write the Summary or Highlights of Your Qualifications

√ Focus on your job objective.
√ Write four or five statements that highlight your strongest qualifications as they relate to the job objective.

1. Repeat your job objective(s):

_____

_____

_____

_____

_____

_____

_____

_____

_____

_____

_____

_____

2. Write five statements that match your qualifications with various aspects of your objectives.

_____

_____

_____

_____

_____

_____

_____

_____

_____

_____

_____

Figure 2-6   The "Never Include" Checklist

There are a number of items that should *not* appear in your resume.
The items include:

Salary requirements.
Compensation requirements are most appropriately discussed at the interview and are rarely mentioned in the resume, unless specifically requested in the ad.

Personal information.
This includes your age, sex, ethnic background, religious or political affiliation, marital status, or children. Also, don't mention weight, height, or other physical characteristics. And don't send a photograph. While this was once considered appropriate, it is rarely done today, and I don't recommend it.

E-mail address.
You may want to include your e-mail address *if and only if* you have a private e-mail account. Never, under any circumstance, use your workplace account. First, there are the ethical and legal issues about use of office systems for personal business. Second, there is the all-important privacy issue. Network administrators or management have access to all office accounts, and you may not care to have your personal e-email scrutinized in this manner. Remember the maxim that the Internet is a postcard, not a letter.

Reference information.
Don't include the names of references or their addresses and telephone numbers. This information is best revealed during the interview when things are getting serious. While some continue to include the phrase "references available upon request" at the bottom of the resume, I recommend dropping it completely. When references are specifically requested in a job announcement or advertisement, include them at the end of the resume.

Information on why you left a position.
Never reveal this on a resume. This information is generally confidential and more appropriately dealt with in the interview.

3 SELECT THE RESUME FORMAT THAT SELLS YOU

Once you have worked out the basic elements of your resume, it is important to find the best possible way to put it all together. No single resume style is ideal in all contexts, so this chapter is devoted to helping you determine which is best for your situation. Three different styles will be considered over the following pages with a focus on the pros, cons, and specific uses of each, making it easy to find the style that is right for you. In addition, we will discuss some special formatting strategies that can be used in specific situations. We will consider, for example, the best styles for someone entering the job market after an extended absence or for someone becoming a librarian at mid-career.

STEP 6: CHOOSE THE BEST RESUME FORMAT

You will choose one of the following formats:

- chronological
- functional
- combination

While experts may disagree about the merits of each of these styles, the important thing is to find the one that is ideally suited

Remember, there is no right
or wrong format—only the
one that demonstrates that
you are best for the job.

to your job objective and the content of your resume. If, after reading this chapter, you cannot settle on one style, try all three and then do a side-by-side comparison to see which one works best for you. In the end, you can only use one, but this exercise will help you make a practical decision. When doing this, try once again to get into your potential employers' heads and think about which style will best reveal your strengths to them. Imagine what you would want to see if you were hiring someone for the job and make your stylistic decisions along these lines. Remember, there is no right or wrong format—only the one that demonstrates that you are best for the job.

To illustrate each of the formats, we're going to leave Janet Taylor for a moment and look at the example of Daryl Jones. We will vary his job objective to demonstrate how each format can be customized to support that particular objective and highlight his most relevant experience.

THE CHRONOLOGICAL RESUME: PROS AND CONS

The most popular of the three formats discussed in this chapter, the chronological resume, is a listing of your work history in reverse order, with your most recent job at the top and your earliest relevant work experience at the bottom.

Pros:

1. It is easily accessible, presenting your information to employers in a way that is immediately comprehensible.
2. It calls attention to job progression, making it particularly useful for showing job promotions and increased responsibility.
3. It can easily reveal that you currently work for a prestigious library or organization.

Cons:

1. The chronological format may be less desirable for those who have been in one position or institution for a long time.
2. It can emphasize gaps in employment.

3. It may give equal weight to all your jobs, highlighting those that may not be as relevant to your job objective.
4. It does not work well for those who are changing careers. If you are looking for a position in a different field of librarianship, it is generally not a good strategy to focus on your current position.
5. If your current job title is vague or does not adequately reflect what you actually do, the chronological format will accentuate this.
6. It does not always highlight your major skill areas.

REVIEWING THE SAMPLE CHRONOLOGICAL RESUME OF DARYL JONES

Daryl's job objective is to work as a project leader for a national program related to the digital preservation of state historical documents and images. He currently works in a prestigious institution, has had steady progression in his field of librarianship, and has some experience related directly to the position he seeks. He particularly wants to draw attention to his current position. Figure 3-1 shows Daryl's resume in the chronological format.

These are the two positions he feels are most relevant to this job objective. His earlier positions will be identified in summary form under a work history heading.

Figure 3-1   Daryl Jones's Chronological Resume Format

Senior Research Librarian, 2001–Present
The Library of Congress, Legislative Reference Service

- Extensive reference service, including in-person assistance, to members of Congress and congressional staff.

- Specialized in public policy issues related to arts and education.

- Expert searching skills using Web and a wide range of databases such as LexisNexis, Westlaw, Factiva, InfoTrac, etc.

- Experienced with archival and special format materials using Library of Congress and other collections related to film, photographs, and music.

- Supervisory experience in delegating and reviewing work of librarians.

Special Assignment, Team Member, User-Evaluation Special Project, 2001-03
The Library of Congress American Image Project

- Evaluated American Image prototype (a Web-based version of archival materials in Library of Congress collections).

- Chaired site selection subcommittee, prepared report, and presented results to senior managers.

- Coordinated orientation and training sessions at Library and at selected sites throughout the U.S.

- Wrote sections of instruction manual, interviewed site coordinators, analyzed site experiences, and was one of three authors of final report.

THE FUNCTIONAL RESUME: PROS AND CONS

Instead of focusing primarily on work history, the functional format calls attention to skills, qualities, and accomplishments. Return to step 4 and select three to four of the skill areas most relevant to the job or position for which you intend to apply. Under each of these skills write a few short sentences describing experiences in your previous positions that showcase the ability in question. These sentences should be as clear and brief as you can make them without sacrificing specificity.

Pros:

1. This format is particularly useful if you have been in one position or one institution for a long time. It focuses on the range of skills and experiences you have acquired there.
2. It works well for those who hope to change careers, since in can be written to call attention to transferable skills. Further, it can downplay one's current position, which may not be relevant to a new career goal.
3. For those reentering the job market or entering it for the first time, this format can be particularly useful, because it provides the opportunity to include volunteer experience in the skills description.
4. Employment gaps are generally less noticeable in this format.
5. This format will deemphasize unstable patterns of employment, such as constant job switching and long periods of part-time or temporary employment.
6. This is one of the best formats for library school students or those with limited job experience.
7. This format allows you to downplay a current job title that may be outdated or that may not adequately reflect your responsibilities.
8. If your jobs are unrelated and don't reveal a distinct career path, this format can instead demonstrate a continuity in your skills and achievements.

Cons:

1. Some employers are suspicious of this format and think

the resume writer may be hiding something (like a major gap in employment).

2. Some consider this format to be less accessible than the chronological format.

REVIEWING THE SAMPLE FUNCTIONAL RESUME OF DARYL JONES

Daryl's job objective has now changed, and he is focusing on a position that is somewhat of a shift from his traditional career path. His objective is to work as a film librarian at the Academy of Motion Picture Arts and Sciences. Although he has worked in a film library, the experience is not recent. Some of his recent experience has been with film research, although it has not been the primary focus of his position.

Figure 3-2 Daryl Jones's Functional Resume Format

Film Reference and Research

- Provided in-person and telephone reference service in a large university film library.
- Created major bibliographies on film history, production, and personalities.
- Examined and prepared special collections inventory of Ritz Radio Theatre disk recordings.
- Excellent research skills with archival and special format material using Library of Congress and external collections related to film, photographs, and music.

Database and Web Skills

- Expert searching skills using Web and a wide range of databases such as LexisNexis, Westlaw, Factiva, InfoTrac, etc.
- Proficient with a wide range of Web tools including HTML and XML coding.
- Designed and updated several pages on Library of Congress Web site.

THE COMBINATION RESUME: PROS AND CONS

As its name suggests, this format is a combination of the two prior styles. Like the chronological format, it uses the applicant's work history as a basis, from most current work to earliest experience. Here, however, skills are listed as the subheadings of each job posting, allowing you to demonstrate the aptitudes you developed or made use of on the job.

Pros:

1. Like the functional format, the combination can be useful if you have been in one position or institution for a long time.
2. Combining styles allows you to indicate distinct jobs without neglecting the skills that will help make you a successful candidate.

Cons:

1. This format is the most difficult to lay out and design, necessitating special attention to visual presentation.

REVIEWING THE SAMPLE COMBINATION RESUME OF DARYL JONES

Assuming once again that Daryl's job objective is to work as a project leader for a national program related to the digital preservation of state historical documents and images, Figure 3-3 shows how the combination format looks.

Figure 3-3   Daryl Jones's Combination Resume Format

Senior Research Librarian, 2001–Present
The Library of Congress, Legislative Reference Service

Reference and Research

- Extensive reference service, including in-person assistance to members of Congress and congressional staff.
- Specialization in issues related to arts and education.
- Experience with archival and special format materials using Library of Congress and other collections related to film, photographs, and music.

Database and Web Skills

- Expert searching skills using the Web and a wide range of databases, such as LexisNexis, Westlaw, Factiva, InfoTrac, etc.
- Proficient with a wide range of Web tools, including HTML and XML coding.
- Designed and updated several pages on Library of Congress Web site.

Special Assignment, Team Member, User-Evaluation Special Project, 2001–03
The Library of Congress American Image Project

Project Evaluation

- Evaluated American Memory prototype (a Web version of archival materials in Library of Congress collections).
- Chaired site selection subcommittee and presented results to senior managers.
- Coordinated orientation and training sessions.

Writing

- Coauthored instruction manual for digital prototype.
- Wrote final report for the project.

You can now see that one of these formats will give you plenty of flexibility to tailor your resume to a specific job objective.

REVIEWING THE SAMPLE COMBINATION RESUME OF JANET TAYLOR

You recall that Janet's job objective is to be a director of a small or medium-size public library. She has been with one institution for a long time, which might suggest that a functional resume would be best. She has held several progressively more responsible positions within her library, however, and she wants to emphasize that fact. Janet has decided that a combination format would best meet her objective (see Figure 3-4). Note how she has listed a main heading for her library that is not repeated with subsequent positions; this helps to emphasize her promotions in one institution. Also, Janet decided that her jobs held prior to 1998 should be listed under an "Additional Work Experience" heading.

Figure 3–4   Janet Taylor's Combination Resume Format

Redford County Public Library District, Redford, AR

Assistant Director, 2002–Present

Management
- Assisted in daily management and administration of over 100 staff members.
- Coordinated transition team to move central library to a new building.
- Chaired Library Building Committee, developed strategic plan, and presented plan to Library Board.
- Wrote comprehensive supervisory manual and library disaster plan.

Technology
- Planned and implemented installation of Dynix automated system.
- Led team which evaluated library systems and made recommendations that were accepted.

Community and Government Relations
- Designed and implemented ADA Strategic Plan.
- Represented library on Redford County Business Development Committee.
- Negotiated building plans with community review board.

Fiscal Management
- Assisted in managing a budget of $4.5 million.
- Co-chaired Audit Review Committee.
- Proposed a budget (2004) which was passed on the first attempt by Library Board.

(continued)

Figure 3-4   Janet Taylor's Combination Resume Format (*Continued*)

Associate Librarian/Head of Technical Services, 1999–2000

Management

- Managed all aspects of Technical Service department including acquisitions, serials, interlibrary loan, and cataloging functions.
- Supervised seven staff members.
- Outstanding performance evaluation.
- Served as Acting Director, 2000.

Cataloging and Technology

- Extensive use of OCLC and the Dynix automated library system.
- Experience with AACR2 and MARC formats.
- Extensive audiovisual cataloging.

Head of Reference, 1998–99

- Supervised a staff of eight reference librarians and four library aides.
- Served on the collection development committee.
- Chaired committee on user access.
- Revised and improved library reference guide.
- Developed and monitored database budget.

THE FUNCTIONAL RESUME STRATEGY FOR CAREER SWITCHERS

If you are like me, you didn't consider librarianship until mid-career. This is certainly not uncommon in our field, but it poses its own set of challenges in terms of marketing yourself and landing your first professional library position. When writing a resume, career switchers frequently find themselves frustrated because they don't want their previous profession to be considered a liability in landing a library job. Sometimes they will not include previous work experience that they consider irrelevant and focus only on limited work or student experience in the field of librarianship.

Instead of minimizing or ignoring previous work experience, think analytically about skills and abilities you acquired in this career that have relevancy to library positions and how you can capitalize on them. This is why step 4 (Identifying Accomplishments and Abilities that Support Each Skill or Quality) should be carefully considered by career-switching resume writers. Also, the qualifications bullets will be very important.

Generally speaking, the functional resume format will work best for the career switcher. It does not emphasize the previous career, but instead focuses on and capitalizes on transferable skills. Don't think of your previous career as a road block, but rather as an additional set of skills and qualifications that will make you even more attractive as a job candidate.

Let's use Francisco Diaz as an example of someone who has completed their MLS and now wants to land their first real library job. Francisco wants to work as a library media specialist and has received his state certification. Prior to making this career switch, Francisco had ten years' experience working as an information technology specialist in the area of commercial banking. In compiling his personal history, Francisco listed the following skill sets and accomplishments to describe his last job with a major commercial bank:

Training

- *Designed, developed, and implemented training to staff on new technology products and business systems.*

> Generally speaking, the functional resume format will work best for the career switcher. It does not emphasize the previous career, but instead focuses on and capitalizes on transferable skills.

SELECT THE RESUME FORMAT THAT SELLS YOU **57**

Management

- *Directed the work of programmers on projects related to customer database and reporting applications.*
- *Managed 6 staff for internal help desk.*

Systems Analysis

- *Developed business requirements for projects including customer statements and privacy.*

Programming

- *Coded, tested, and implemented programs for projects.*

You can quickly see that Francisco has a wealth of skills that will be easily transferable to the field of librarianship and as a library media specialist, in particular. These include technology proficiencies, ability to work with people, excellent writing skills, and project management.

Having completed an analysis of his previous career, Francisco develops the following qualifications statement:

SUMMARY OF QUALIFICATIONS

- Certified library media specialist
- Working knowledge of a wide range of technologies
- Proven organizational and leadership skills
- Excellent writing and presentation skills

If you are a career-switcher, take a close look at the functional resumes in the following chapters for additional ideas on how to structure your resume.

You've made remarkable progress! Having chosen your resume format, you're ready to pull all the pieces together and to write the first draft.

PUT IT ALL TOGETHER

In this chapter we bring together all of the elements worked out in previous steps and assemble the actual resume. Once this is done, we will go over a series of stylistic tips to make sure that your resume looks as attractive, clean, and appealing as possible. Finally, we will introduce the chapters containing sample resumes.

STEP 7: ASSEMBLE THE RESUME

With six steps under your belt, you have done most of the hard work, but try not to lose your concentration. You have all the building blocks, and now is the time to assemble them. In this section, we will look at the arrangement of the major headings of the resume.

FIVE GENERAL GUIDELINES

Here are some general guidelines to follow as we consider each part:

1. List precise details and examples. Avoid repetitive detail. Remember the maxim of the great architect Mies van der Rohe: "Less is more."
2. Use plain English—avoid flowery language, arcane professional jargon, and acronyms that are not universally recognized.
3. Use bold face and/or all capital letters for each heading.
4. Separate each heading with two or three spaces.
5. Remove periods from the end of headings. If you choose to place periods at the end of bulleted statements, be consistent throughout.

> Use plain English — avoid flowery language, arcane professional jargon, and acronyms that are not universally recognized.

LIST HEADINGS AND INSERT INFORMATION

Here's where all your hard work in the previous chapters bears fruit. Think of your answers as building blocks, separated by headings.

HEADING 1: NAME AND ADDRESS

This consists of:

1. Your name prominently displayed in capital letters, in boldface and/or in the largest font size used in the resume.
2. Your address may be your home address, work address, or both. Note: Placing your office address at the top of the resume calls attention to your current institution. This may be to your advantage, especially if the organization is well regarded and you are using the functional format (see Figure 9-8). On the other hand, if receiving correspondence at your office is a problem, use only your home address.
3. Phone numbers may include home, cell phone, and office phone numbers. Omit the office number if a call from a prospective employer would be embarrassing or otherwise problematic.
4. E-mail address should only include your private e-mail address, as there are a variety of ethical issues and privacy concerns attached to the personal use of work e-mail accounts.

Here is Janet Taylor's name and address heading:

> JANET F. TAYLOR
> 27 Chelsea Court
> Woodland Springs, AR 72764
> Home: (501) 555–2828 Office: (501) 555-1415
> e-mail: Jtaylor@aol.com

HEADING 2: THE JOB OBJECTIVE

The job objective, as worked out in step 2, is placed immediately under the heading and may be bolded.

Here is Janet Taylor's job objective:

> Objective: Position as director in a small or medium-size public library.

Don't forget, this statement should be concise and to the point! Also, be sure to keep the objective in mind as you finish assembling the resume, checking to make sure that it is fully supported by the contents of the later sections.

HEADING 3: QUALIFICATIONS

Open this section with one of the following headings

- Summary of Qualifications,
- Highlights of Qualifications, or simply,
- Qualifications.

This section should contain no more than five items, each as clear and concise as possible. Separate the different items with bullets.

Here are Janet Taylor's qualifications:

> SUMMARY OF QUALIFICATIONS
>
> - Outstanding supervisory and administrative skills gained in dynamic, medium-size public library.
> - Extensive experience in evaluation and implementation of library systems.
> - Assisted in the management of a budget of over $ 4 million.
> - Proven skills in government and community relations.

HEADING 4: WORK EXPERIENCE USING CHRONOLOGICAL OR COMBINATION FORMATS

This heading will vary depending on which resume format you have chosen.

When employing either the chronological or combination formats, one of the three following headings generally works well:

- Experience,
- Work Experience, or
- Work History.

Under the heading, provide the following information for each item:

- job title,
- beginning and end years of employment, and
- name of organization and location.

In Figure 4-1, Janet, using the combination format, looks back at the work she did in step 4. She lists her positions, the appropriate functional headings under each position, and one-line statements to support each heading. She constantly checks to make sure each one-liner relates to her job objective.

Figure 4-1   Janet Taylor's Work Experience in Combination Format

Redford County Public Library District, Redford, AR

Assistant Director, 2002–present

Management
- Assisted in daily management and administration of over 100 staff members.
- Coordinated transition team to move central library to a new building.
- Chaired Library Building Committee, developed strategic plan, and presented plan to Library Board.
- Wrote comprehensive supervisory manual and library disaster plan.

Technology
- Planned and implemented installation of Dynix automated system.
- Led team which evaluated library systems and made recommendations that were accepted.

Community and Government Relations
- Designed and implemented ADA Strategic Plan.
- Represented library on Redford County Business Development Committee.
- Negotiated building plans with community review board.

Fiscal Management
- Assisted in managing a budget of $4.5 million.
- Co-chaired Audit Review Committee.
- Proposed a budget (2004) which was passed on the first attempt by Library Board.

(continued)

Figure 4-1 Janet Taylor's Work Experience in Combination Format (*Continued*)

Associate Librarian/Head of Technical Services, 1999–2000

Management

- Managed all aspects of Technical Service Department including acquisitions, serials, interlibrary loan, and cataloging functions.
- Supervised seven staff members.
- Outstanding performance evaluation.

Cataloging and Technology

- Extensive use of OCLC and the Dynix automated library system.
- Experience with AACR2 and MARC formats.
- Extensive audiovisual cataloging.

Head of Reference, 1998–99

- Supervised a staff of eight reference librarians and four library aides.
- Served on the collection development committee.
- Chaired committee on user access.
- Revised and improved library reference guide.
- Developed and monitored database budget.

When using the chronological or combination formats, focus on only the most relevant of your positions, and provide selective details. Do not describe all of your past jobs. How relevant is that pizza delivery job you had in college to the library directorship job you're pursuing today?

HEADING 5: WORK EXPERIENCE USING THE FUNCTIONAL FORMAT

When employing the functional format, use one of the following headings:

- Experience,
- Skills and Experience, or
- Skills and Accomplishments.

After the functional headings and one-liners, follow with a section called "Work History" or "Work Experience."

Figure 4-2 shows Janet Taylor's work experience had she chosen the functional format.

Figure 4–2   Janet Taylor's Work Experience in Functional Format

WORK EXPERIENCE

Redford County Public Library District, Redford, AR
- Assistant Director, 2001–present
- Acting Director, 2000
- Associate Librarian/Head of Technical Services, 1999–2000
- Head of Reference, 1998–99

San Angelo Free Public Library, San Angelo, TX
- Reference Librarian, 1994–97

Sam Houston Elementary School, Eagle Pass, TX
- School Librarian, 1992–94

When using either of these two resume formats, you should not feel obligated to give descriptions for all of your past jobs. Focus instead on only the most relevant of your positions, selectively providing details where they will be helpful.

HEADING 6: ADDITIONAL WORK EXPERIENCE

If it feels important to list less relevant jobs, provide very short summaries under an "Additional Work Experience" later in the resume.

ADDITIONAL WORK EXPERIENCE

- Reference Librarian, San Angelo Free Public Library, 1994-97.
- Elementary School Librarian, Sam Houston Elementary School, Eagle Pass, TX, 1992-94.

HEADING 7: EDUCATION

This heading generally appears simply as "Education." Under the heading, in reverse chronological order, list the following:

- degree awarded,
- school and location,
- year of degree,
- major,
- honors (cum laude, summa cum laude, etc.).

Generally, degree acronyms such as B.A., B.S., and M.A. are understood by most resume readers. For the nonlibrarian reader, however, you may want to list Master of Library Science as opposed to M.L.S. For degrees that are not commonly known, always spell them out—don't make the reader guess.

Here is Janet Taylor's education:

EDUCATION

M.S. in Library Science, University of North Texas, Denton, TX, 1994.
B.A., Grinnell College, IA, 1990. Major in sociology; minor in French.

HEADING 8: PROFESSIONAL INVOLVEMENT

List professional organization involvement under one of the following headings:

- Professional Organizations,
- Professional Association Involvement, or
- Professional Activities.

As we discussed earlier, don't just list memberships. If you have been actively involved in an association, be sure to indicate it. The functional format lends itself well to highlighting transferable skills and experience you have gained in professional associations.

Here is Janet Taylor's professional involvement:

> **PROFESSIONAL ASSOCIATION INVOLVEMENT**
>
> American Library Association, 1993–present
> - Supervisory Skills Committee, Library and Administration and Management Association. Helped to establish a listserv on supervisory skills and assisted with the planning and implementation of annual conference program, "First Line Supervisors: On the Edge."
>
> Arkansas Library Association, 1989–present
> - Member, 50th Anniversary Committee. Served on a team that planned association events for celebration. This included a Tribute Day event involving Arkansas legislators and media.
> - Secretary, 1989–90.

HEADING 9: ADDITIONAL HEADINGS

If relevant, include the following headings:

- Awards or Honors,
- Publications,
- Presentations, and/or
- Research and Grant Activities.

HEADING 10: VOLUNTEER WORK AND PERSONAL INTERESTS

These can be listed as:

- Volunteer Work,
- Volunteer Activities,
- Volunteer Experience,
- Personal Interests,
- Personal Activities,
- Volunteer Work/Personal Interests, or
- Other Activities.

Here are Janet Taylor's volunteer work and personal interests:

VOLUNTEER WORK/PERSONAL INTERESTS

- Reading is Fun program volunteer, 2000–1. Tutored elementary school children on weekends.
- Volunteer coordinator, St. Mary Parish, 2002. Organized volunteer visits to three nursing and long-term care facilities.
- Embroidery, rollerblading, travel, French language group.

PROOFREAD! PROOFREAD! PROOFREAD!

Be sure to allow sufficient time to proofread your resume several times over the course of several days. You'll be amazed to discover errors even after three or four reviews. Ask someone else skilled in proofreading to review for grammar, punctuation, and spelling. I can't overemphasize the importance of perfect spelling. Most employers are sticklers for this and will dismiss a resume with a typo. Their assumption is that if you can't get it right in a resume, you won't get it right in your everyday work. Susan Kreimer, a contributing writer for the *Washington Post*, reports, "In a recent survey of state agency human resource directors, 88 percent said accuracy in writing was 'extremely important;' 71 percent also gave the same weight to spelling, grammar, and punctuation." (*Washington Post*, July 24, 2005, p. K1)

> Be sure to allow sufficient time to proofread your resume several times over the course of several days. You'll be amazed to discover errors even after three or four reviews.

STEP 8: ASSESS THE LOOK OF YOUR RESUME

Up to this point we have dealt primarily with the *substance* of the resume. Now it's time to examine how it *looks*. Well-tailored language won't mean a thing if the resume doesn't have curbside appeal—i.e., an attractive format that is easy to read. In this section, we will consider the following elements to ensure that your resume looks visually appealing:

- resume length,
- formats and computer tips for graphics, and
- paper.

DETERMINING THE LENGTH

This is one of the most debated resume questions. One page? Two pages? Three or longer? Everyone seems to have a different perspective. There is no hard-and-fast rule—each individual is different, and so is each resume. A one-page resume is ideal—the reader can quickly review it and capture the "big picture." Don't limit yourself to one page, however, if it means that you must reduce the margins to the point where there is no white space on the page or the type size becomes so minuscule that you need a magnifying glass to read it. That said, depending on your background, experience, and career level, one page simply will not be enough in many cases. Generally speaking, a two-page resume will not cost you any points. In the event that your resume pages become separated, be sure to put your name on the second page. But do think carefully before you go to a third page; review carefully to make sure every element is absolutely necessary. Remember that your resume may be one of several hundred being reviewed, and the employer will spend only seconds with it.

One exception to this rule is the Curriculum Vitae (CV), which is more popular and often required in academic institutions. The CV will include detailed information about publications, courses taught, and the like, and therefore requires greater length. (see Figure 7-4)

CREATING THE FORMAT ON YOUR COMPUTER

Let's start off with some guidelines to give your format a professional appearance:

- Use "bullets" for lists—they create a clear, graphic image and are easy to follow.
- Put headings in **bold**. It's easier for the eye to move from one section to the next.
- Make sure you have lots of **white** space on the pages. Don't shrink your margins and fill every inch of paper with text. Leaving white spaces makes it easier to read.
- Choose a traditional and conservative typeface that is simple and dignified. Avoid script, old English, or any "creative" typeface.
- Use *italics* for headings and for names of journals, but employ these features with restraint.
- Vary the typeface as little as possible. Type size should be easily readable—resist the temptation to use small type.

Now, take some time to review the sample resumes included in this book in Chapters 5 through 9. You will observe various styles

> Make sure you have lots of white space on the pages. Don't shrink your margins and fill every inch of paper with text. Leaving white spaces makes it easier to read.

of format and organization, each of which gives a distinctive look, yet is easy to read and visually pleasing. Again, you don't need fancy desktop publishing or graphics packages to achieve a professional look. All of the resumes in these chapters were completed on my home PC using WordPerfect.

In reviewing the sample resumes, you will note the use of graphic lines, *italics*, and **bold** to add visual appeal. With WordPerfect 12, I created horizontal and vertical lines by selecting: Insert> Line> Custom> Line Styles. A wide range of options are available. Similar options are available in Word.

Use graphic features sparingly, and remember: "Less is more." Too many graphics can detract from the content of the resume. For positions requiring an artistic bent, something more creative may be appropriate, but use novel or unique formats with great caution. The goal is to find just the right balance.

SELECTING THE RIGHT PAPER

Consult a stationery store for a good selection of paper and follow some general guidelines:

The paper should be:

- of excellent quality,
- white or cream color (*never* colored paper, which looks unprofessional and will not photocopy well should the resume reader decide to share it with someone else),
- hard finish containing significant cotton content,
- decent heft with a nice feel (avoid textured papers, since print quality may be uneven with certain types of printers), and
- available, if possible, with a matching 9" x 11" envelope, to allow you to send the resume without folding it.

If possible, use a good quality laser printer, not a dot matrix. Avoid photocopying a resume and resist faxing it. Remember that the employer may show it to someone else, and a fax doesn't make the best presentation. If a potential employer needs it quickly, use an overnight delivery service. Don't use double-sided copies for resumes; the reader may neglect to turn it over.

OK. Drum roll, please. See Figure 4-3 to discover how Janet's final resume turned out:

Figure 4-3 Janet Taylor's Final "After" Resume

JANET F. TAYLOR

27 Chelsea Court

Woodland Springs, AR 72764

Home: (501) 770-2828 Office: (501) 770-1415

E-mail: jtaylor@aol.com

Objective: Position as Director in a small or medium-size public library.

SUMMARY OF QUALIFICATIONS

- Outstanding supervisory and administrative skills gained in dynamic, medium-sized public library.
- Extensive experience in evaluation and implementation of library technologies.
- Assisted in the management a budget of over $4 million.
- Proven skills in government and community relations.

WORK EXPERIENCE

Redford County Public Library District, Redford, AR

Assistant Director, 2002–present

Management
- Assisted in daily management and administration of over 100 staff members.
- Coordinated transition team to move central library to a new building.
- Chaired Library Building Committee, developed strategic plan, and presented plan to Library Board.
- Wrote comprehensive supervisory manual and library disaster plan.

(continued)

Figure 4-3   Janet Taylor's Final "After" Resume (*Continued*)

Technology
- Planned and implemented installation of Dynix automated system.
- Led team which evaluated library systems and made recommendation which was accepted.

Community and Government Relations
- Designed and implemented ADA Strategic Plan.
- Represented library on Redford County Business Development Committee.
- Negotiated building plans with community review board.

Fiscal Management
- Assisted in managing a budget of $4.5 million.
- Cochaired Audit Review Committee.
- Proposed a budget (2004) which was passed on the first attempt by Library Board.

Associate Librarian/Head of Technical Services, 1999–2000

Management
- Managed all aspects of Technical Service Department including acquisitions, serials, interlibrary loan, and cataloging functions.
- Supervised seven staff members.
- Outstanding performance evaluation.
- Served as Acting Director 2000.

Cataloging and Technology
- Extensive use of OCLC and the Dynix automated library system.
- Experience with AACR2 and MARC formats.
- Extensive audiovisual cataloging.

Janet Taylor, p. 2.

(continued)

Figure 4-3 Janet Taylor's Final "After" Resume (*Continued*)

Head of Reference, 1998–99

- Supervised a staff of eight reference librarians and four library aides.
- Served on the collection development committee.
- Chaired committee on user access.
- Revised and improved library reference guide.
- Developed and monitored database budget.

ADDITIONAL WORK EXPERIENCE

Reference Librarian, San Angelo Free Public Library, 1994-97.

Elementary School Librarian, Sam Houston Elementary School, Eagle Pass, TX, 1992-94.

EDUCATION

M.S. in Library Science, University of North Texas, Denton, TX, 1994.

B.A., Grinnell College, Grinnell, IA, 1990. Major in sociology; minor in Italian. Member of Student Council and Choral Choir.

PROFESSIONAL ASSOCIATION INVOLVEMENT

American Library Association, 1993–present
- Supervisory Skills Committee, Library Administration and Management Association. Helped to establish a listserv on supervisory skills and assisted with the planning and implementation of annual conference program: "First Line Supervisors: On the Edge."

Arkansas Library Association, 1989–present
- Member, 50th Anniversary Committee. Served on a team which planned Association events for celebration. This included a Tribute Day event involving Arkansas legislators and media.
- Secretary, 1989-90.

VOLUNTEER WORK/PERSONAL INTERESTS

- Reading is Fun program volunteer, 2000-01. Tutored elementary schoolchildren on weekends.
- Volunteer coordinator, St. Mary Parish, 2002. Organized volunteer visits to three nursing and long-term care facilities.
- Embroidery, rollerblading, travel, French language group.

This is quite a contrast to Janet's original resume! All of the problems we originally noted have been addressed. The look is crisp and professional, with graphics lines adding visual interest. Janet has also included her name at the top of page 2 in the event the pages become separated.

STEP 9: CONDUCT A FINAL CHECKLIST

Whew! You've come a long way. Before you turn it over to your potential employer, though, let's review the following checklist to make sure it is picture perfect:

1. Did you proofread your resume repeatedly? Have you checked and rechecked grammar, spelling, and punctuation?
2. Is it neat and clean? Coffee rings and potato chip stains don't belong here.
3. Have you taken time for a reality check by letting someone else review it? Choose among the following individuals to give you this critical feedback:

   - peers,
   - mentors,
   - managers,
   - someone who doesn't know you well (you'll often get the most valuable insights here),
   - someone who hires in the field of your job objective,
   - people outside of the field of librarianship (they will be quick to question vague language or unfamiliar acronyms), and
   - if you are an unsuccessful candidate for a job and have an opportunity to follow up with the interviewer, ask for suggestions on how your resume could be improved.

4. Have you described your positions in your own words? Did you avoid phrases like "duties included" or "responsible for"? Using language from formal job descriptions is not acceptable.
5. Have you included relevant nonprofessional work experience and volunteer work? Don't underestimate these when they are germane to your job objective.

6. Have you accounted for periods of unemployment? Remember that resume readers are always alert to this.
7. Have you used acronyms that will have no meaning for the employer? Only use those that are universally known.
8. Will your resume pass the *New York Times* test? In other words, have you written anything you wouldn't want published on the front page of a newspaper?
9. Is your resume concise and to the point?
10. Is there plenty of white space? Is it easy to read?
11. Have you checked and rechecked to make sure that every statement in your resume supports your job objective?
12. Have you carefully proofed for typos? And be sure there are absolutely no handwritten corrections!

If you have answered "yes" to all of the above questions, you have produced a job-winning resume. Congratulations!

SAMPLE RESUMES TO CONSIDER

The next five chapters provide a wide range of sample resumes of "real life" librarians (with names and places changed). They have been organized in broad categories of *target* positions:

Chapter 5: Management and Nonmanagement Technology/Systems Librarian
Chapter 6: Nonsupervisory Librarian
Chapter 7: Supervisory/Management Librarian
Chapter 8: Recent Graduate of Library School Program
Chapter 9: Special Librarian

Each chapter contains the actual resumes. In addition you will find:

- special tips about the particular job category,
- a listing by name of each resume,
- a description of the individual's job objective,
- background on the position for which they are applying, and
- details about how the individual tailored his or her resume, including special techniques used, why one format was chosen over another, and other unique features.

The examples cover a wide range of jobs in libraries and represent many different types of libraries and organizations, such as:

- academic,
- public,
- school,
- association,
- private companies,
- foundations, and
- government agencies, etc.

They also represent individuals at many different career stages, with each resume tailored for a position in that particular job category. Pay particular attention to the ways in which candidates with experience describe their work when they target jobs in different areas of librarianship.

Part II

Reviewing Successful Sample Resumes

5 SAMPLE RESUMES: MANAGEMENT AND NONMANAGEMENT TECHNOLOGY/SYSTEMS LIBRARIAN

TIPS FOR THE SAVVY RESUME WRITER

- Technology has revolutionized the library, and librarians with skills in these areas are in great demand. Technology/systems librarian positions are an exciting and growing area of librarianship—a good place to build your career.
- Employers always look for workers with specialized knowledge. Don't limit yourself only to specific knowledge of various databases, systems, and networks. Employers are also looking for individuals who are flexible and adaptable.
- Document skills that demonstrate your ability to adjust to change and to seek out new trends, solutions, and products.
- Be especially wary of system acronyms. While many acronyms are well known (MARC, OCLC, LAN, LexisNexis, etc.) in the profession, others are more obscure. When in doubt, spell it out, or describe it so the employer won't have to guess.
- Describe your experience with a system in detail.
- Ask yourself every question imaginable: Were you involved in the planning stage of the system? Did you serve on or head a committee to look at the feasibility of installing a network? Did you work with vendors in the planning or implementation stage? How extensive was your involvement? Did you make recommendations? Were you responsible for selecting the system? Did you receive training on this system? Did you train others? Did you receive any type of certification? Did you work with users directly? Did you plan or implement training? Did you do a survey? A feasibility study? A cost analysis? Did you prepare a report?

- Define your accomplishments in terms of results. How did your technology solution improve service, enhance operations, streamline a process, or save time?
- Be sure to emphasize the "human element." A frequent criticism of technology staff is that while they may have excellent technical abilities, they don't have adequate people skills. If you have led committees or worked closely with users, be sure to indicate that. Emphasize any significant work that you did in surveying users or getting feedback.

MEET THE CANDIDATES

Benjamin Bradshaw is seeking a leadership position in the area of digitization. Notice how well the work experience heading is designed using the combo format (see Figure 5-1). For example, his position as rare book digitization specialist is clearly documented to focus on his significant experience with technology and administration.

Brian Lavelle has just lost his job as a senior manager of an information center due to the abolishment of a state agency. His goal is to find a similar position in the private sector. His job progression in the agency was impressive, and he developed solid skills. To highlight these attributes, he chooses the chronological format (see Figure 5-2). His qualifications statement is especially well-written.

Michelle C. Gallo has served in three positions in one organization. They have involved progressively more responsibility and reinforced her job goal: a position as a university electronic information resources librarian. Her one-line statements are very focused on supporting her job objective (see Figure 5-3).

Pamela G. Robinson has built a career focused on library technology, first as a consultant and later in a public library and as a director of a Web index. Her resume reflects her steady and impressive career progression (see Figure 5-4). She now seeks a major leadership position in technology in a large urban library system.

Steven R. Kratz seeks a position as a director for systems in a large university. He has a good range of experience in several different jobs and chooses the chronological format to market himself (see Figure 5-5). Note that Steven defines lesser-known acronyms, like MELNET, which are not readily identifiable to most employers.

Jack DiNardo has significant Web-related experience that he thinks will serve him well in a more senior technology position (see Figure 5-6). He successfully quantifies his experience under the work experience heading.

Deborah Delong is looking for a position as head of systems in a large public or academic library. Although she has published and spoken extensively, she is selective in choosing publications and presentations so as to limit her resume to two pages. She chooses the chronological format to emphasize her current position as Assistant Head of Systems (see Figure 5-7). Note the italicized headings.

Alice Fay Kelly has acquired special expertise in the private sector in the area of e-commerce and wants to capitalize on this experience for her next position in a major corporate library (see Figure 5-8). She makes good use of the presentations section to demonstrate her expertise.

Figure 5-1   Sample Technology/Systems Librarian Resume: Bradshaw

BENJAMIN BRADSHAW

1631 Fourteenth St. • New Haven, CT 06520
Office: 203.441.2326 • bbradshaw@access.com

OBJECTIVE: To manage a large and complex digitization project in a rare book environment.

SUMMARY OF QUALIFICATIONS

- Expert knowledge of all aspects of digitization of rare materials.
- Ability to manage complex technology projects within budget and on time.
- Experienced supervisor and administrator.
- Excellent interpersonal skills and experience in making presentations.

WORK EXPERIENCE

Beincke Rare Book & Manuscript Library, Yale University, New Haven, CT

Rare Book Digitization Specialist, 2002–present

Technology
- Oversaw major digitization project involving presentation, display, conservation, preservation rehousing, image capture, and cataloging of rare books and documents.
- Drafted complex instructions for image capture and text conversion.
- Completed conversion of over 200,000 digital files.
- Assessed and approved collections for digitization.

Administration
- Led team of ten staff.
- Developed and oversaw budgets for several digitization contracts exceeding $1 million.
- Lectured frequently on the Beincke's digitization project.
- Hired several librarians.

Computer Technician, 1998–02

Digitization
- Contributed content to *Selection and Priorization: Categories, Content and Guidelines*.
- Coordinated public service digitization requests.
- Identified standards for image quality as well as metadata.
- Assisted in development of inventory plan.

Cataloging
- Completed cataloging of major Victorian era sheet music collection.
- Trained new cataloging staff on Beincke policies and procedures.
- Wrote training manuals for new catalogers.
- Advised managers about a wide range of cataloging issues in the library.

(continued)

Figure 5-1 Sample Technology/Systems Librarian Resume: Bradshaw (*Continued*)

Benjamin Bradshaw, Page 2

EDUCATION

M.L.S., State University of New York, Albany, 1996.
M.F.A., Writing and Literature, Hunter College, New York, NY, 1994.
B.A., Psychology, Emory University, Atlanta, GA, 1992.

PUBLICATIONS

"Computer-Assisted Instruction: Is It an Option for Bibliographic Instruction in Large Undergraduate Survey Classes" in *College and Research Libraries*, 59, no. 1, January 2003): 19–27.

"The Psychology of Learning and Cognitive Styles—Practical Implications for Teaching," *Learning to Teach—Workshops on Instructions*. Edited by the Learning to Teach Task Force, Bibliographic Instruction Section, Association of College and Research Libraries, American Library Association, Chicago 2003.

"Mentoring Science Students," *Special Libraries* 85, no. 4, Fall, 2002.

Frequent book review contributor to *Library Quarterly*, and *Library Journal*.

Currently writing a book entitled *Emerging Technologies and the Library*, for Hayworth Press.

(continued)

Figure 5-1   Sample Technology/Systems Librarian Resume: Bradshaw (*Continued*)

Benjamin Bradshaw, Page 3

PRESENTATIONS

"Electronic Exhibitions in Special Collections," Rare Book and Manuscript Annual Preconference, Columbia University, New York, NY, 2005.

Have lectured extensively on behalf of the Beincke Library on topics related to digitization and book exhibitions. Selected lectures include:
- National Library of China (2005)
- Royal Dutch Library (2004)
- Instituto Ravignani, Buenos Aires, Argentina (2003)
- The French-American Foundation, Paris (2003)

Expert consultant on development of digital collections of materials relating to historic landscape architecture: Bard Graduate Center for Studies in the Decorative Arts, Design, and Culture, New York, NY, 2002.

RESEARCH AND GRANT ACTIVITIES

- ALA/ACRL Institute on Information Literacy Immersion Program—member of founding faculty responsible for developing curriculum for inaugural program and presenting instruction at first Immersion Program in 2000, Plattsburg, NY.

- Harvard University Office of Instruction Development Improvement Programs grant for development of a computer-assisted instruction program to teach undergraduate psychology students the organization of and access to journal material in the life sciences, 2003–04.

PROFESSIONAL ACTIVITIES

American Library Association

   ALA Office of Accreditation—Site team member for External Accreditation Review for the University of Washington, 2004.

Association of College and Research Libraries, Bibliographic Instruction Section
   Learning to Teach Task Force, 2002–03.
   Education for Bibliographic Instruction Committee, 2001.

New Members Round Table
   Chair, Nominating Committee, 2000–01.
   Director for Membership, Awards and Continuing Education Committees, 1999–2000.
   EBSCO Scholarship Committee Chair, 1998–99.

Member: American Psychological Association, Medical Library Group of Massachusetts, Phi Beta Mu, Social and Behavioral Sciences Librarians Network.

Figure 5-2 Sample Technology/Systems Librarian Resume: Lavelle

BRIAN LAVELLE
22 N. Oak St. #7
Newark, NJ 07102
973.422.3134
E-MAIL: blavelle@wellspring.net

CAREER OBJECTIVE: A senior position in information services or management using proven administrative skills to increase and improve the productivity of a library.

SUMMARY OF QUALIFICATIONS

- Expertise and leadership skills in managing an electronic information center.
- Over 14 years of experience in developing staff and resources in information services.
- Extensive experience in implementing new technologies.
- Strong communication skills.

PROFESSIONAL EXPERIENCE

New Jersey Department of Technology Research, Newark, NJ

Manager, Information Services, 1999–present
- Supervised staff of 8 (including 4 librarians).
- Responded to over 1,400 requests a month.
- Prepared and monitored $325K budget for all salary and materials.
- Provided reference services in a networked IBM environment.
- Evaluated and implemented new technologies.
- Hired and trained all personnel.
- Served as network supervisor in a Novell LAN environment.

Assistant Manager, Information Services, 1995–99
- Coordinated all reference services.
- Supervised and performed online searches using PubMed MEDLINE, LexisNexis, InfoTrac, Factiva, ProQuest, etc.
- Supervised Interlibrary Loan system and electronic mail network.
- Assisted in development and maintenance of automated acquisitions, catalog, and circulation systems.
- Maintained and interpreted statistics for management reports.
- Indexed and abstracted Department of Technology Research reports for inclusion in NTIS database.
- Trained department staff on online services to improve productivity.

(continued)

Figure 5-2   Sample Technology/Systems Librarian Resume: Lavelle (*Continued*)

Brian L. Lavelle   Page 2

National Oil and Gas Institute, Washington, D.C. 1997–99

Information Specialist
- Performed wide range of reference services to staff and members of the association.
- Acquired excellent knowledge of technical and business information sources.
- Coordinated publication of Institute calendar and Information Directory.

ADDITIONAL WORK EXPERIENCE

Rutgers University, Mathematical Sciences Library, New Brunswick, NJ
- Librarian, Acquisitions/Serials Department, 1996-97
- Librarian, Information Services Department, 1996

AT & T Laboratories Technical Library, Piscataway, NJ
- Reference Intern, 1995

EDUCATION

Certificate of Completion, Special Libraries Association Middle Management units in Management Skills, Marketing and Public Relations, Human Resources, and Analytical Tools, 2004.

M.L.I.S., Department of Library and Information Science, Rutgers University, New Brunswick, NJ, 1996.

B.S., Biology, Lesley College, Cambridge, MA, 1993.

PROFESSIONAL AFFILIATIONS

Member: American Library Association, Special Libraries Association.

Figure 5-3   Sample Technology/Systems Librarian Resume: Gallo

Michelle C. Gallo
1217 Grange St.
Indianapolis, IN 46205
Office: 817.244.3596   Home: 817.423.3425
E-mail: gallo@msn.com

Objective: To serve as Electronic Information Resources Librarian at the Life Sciences Library, University of Indiana, Bloomington.

Summary of Qualifications

- Experience in planning and implementing technology in a library.
- Strong communication and organizational skills.
- Excellent knowledge of a wide range of online services.
- Extensive experience working in a scientific environment.

Work Experience

Indiana Department of Health, Indianapolis, IN

Technical Information Specialist, 2002–present
- Researched and responded to reference inquiries from state health officials.
- Monitored health related legislation in the Indiana Assembly.
- Performed extensive online searches specializing in health databases.
- Attended and reviewed state Assembly committee meetings on health issues.

Public Information Specialist, 2001
- Responded to over 50 public inquiries each day, primarily by telephone.
- Assigned requests to health specialists within the Department of Health.
- Served on committee which implemented a network.

Serials Technician, 2000
- Assisted in the conversion of automated serials control to a new system.
- Created database records, tracked serial receipts, and performed software maintenance.

Systems Librarian, Texas Woman's University, Denton, TX, 1999

- Maintained ProCite database of 1180 rare (pre-1850) titles.
- Performed extensive online and Web searches.
- Installed and maintained library software.
- Managed monograph and serial acquisitions.
- Wrote and edited grant proposals for library funding.

(continued)

Figure 5-3 Sample Technology/Systems Librarian Resume: Gallo (*Continued*)

Michelle C. Gallo, Page 2

Freelance Work

Writer and Translator, 1998–2001
- Wrote film/theater reviews and natural history articles.
- Edited community events and entertainment calendars.
- Created brochures and flyers.
- Translated news features from English into Spanish, French, and German.

Courseware Consultant, 2000
Kodak International Center for Training and Management Development, Rochester, NY
- Designed and developed telecommunications training package for marketing representatives.
- Supervised staff of 3 programmers.

Professional Associations

Special Libraries Association
- Treasurer, Student Chapter, Texas Woman's University, 1998.
- Member, Student Affiliation and Scholarship Committee, 1997.
- Member, Pamphlet Task Force, Natural History Caucus, 1997.

Education

M.A. in Library Science, Texas Woman's University, Denton, TX, 1998. Received Beta Mu Scholarship.

B.A., University of Indiana, Bloomington, IN, 1996. Magna cum laude, Phi Beta Kappa. Major in Spanish. Coursework at the Universidad Complutense de Madrid.

Figure 5-4 Sample Technology/Systems Librarian Resume: Robertson

PAMELA G. ROBERTSON

2471 New Windsor Ave.
Swampscott, MA 01097
571.242.3731   pgrob@earthlink.net

OBJECTIVE: Leadership position in technology in a large urban library system.

QUALIFICATIONS

- Extensive experience related to Web site production and administration.
- Broad knowledge of technology applications for libraries and educators.
- Demonstrated experience in budget and personnel administration.
- Nationally recognized for publications related to the Internet.

PROFESSIONAL EXPERIENCE

Director, Educators' Web Index (ewi.org), Newton, MA, 2000–present

- Initiated and implemented major systems conversion including funding, vendor selection, overseeing database design, code testing and communication plan.
- Editor of weekly newsletter with subscription of over 30,000.
- Developed major marketing campaign to libraries including radio spots and in-person demonstrations.
- Planned budget, wrote grant proposals, and successfully doubled funding.
- Managed eight librarians and worked with advisory board.

Director of Technology, Elgin Park Public Library System, Elgin Park, IL, 1998–2000

- Introduced many new technologies, including remote databases, wireless technology, and e-books.
- Supervised staff of ten librarians and programmers.
- Oversaw all aspects of NT server and related applications.
- Administered budget of over $2 million.

Consultant, Road Less Traveled, Inc., Boston, MA, 1997-98

- Advised public libraries on a wide range of issues related to the Internet.
- Wrote articles on the Internet for professional publications.
- Developed policies and practices on filtering.
- Consulted with several professional library associations.

EDUCATION

Master of Library Science, State University of New York, Albany, 1996.

B.A., Psychology, Mary Washington College, Fredericksburg, VA, 1992.

(continued)

Figure 5-4   Sample Technology/Systems Librarian Resume: Robertson (*Continued*)

Pamela G. Robertson, *Page 2*

PROFESSIONAL ACTIVITIES

American Library Association
- Member, Web Advisory Committee, 2003–present.
- Chair, Design Subcommittee, 2004–present.
- Member-at-large, ALA Council, 2002–present.

Massachusetts Library Association
- Founding member, MLA Gay and Lesbian Task Force, 1997.
- Electronic Meeting Task Force, 1996–97.

SELECTED PUBLICATIONS

The 21st Century Web: Challenges for Librarians, New Canaan, CT: Avanti Press, 2005.

"Everything You Need to Know About Filters," *The Internet Educator*, April 2004, pp. 24–29.

"Managing Volunteers," *Non-Profits Today*, June 2005.

Frequent contributor to a wide range of library and education journals.

AWARDS AND HONORS

Alumni Leadership Award, State University of New York, Albany, 1995.

"Best Article of the Year," *The Bottom Line*, 2004.

Figure 5-5 Sample Technology/Systems Librarian Resume: Kratz

STEVEN R. KRATZ

Division of Library Development and Services
Missouri Department of Education
Jefferson City, MO 65102
573.525.3245 srkratz@zipnet.com

JOB OBJECTIVE: Systems Director for the Library, University of Arkansas.

QUALIFICATIONS

- Expert knowledge of networks and networked environments.
- Experienced in coordinating technology in a university environment.
- Extensive administrative and supervisory experience.
- Excellent skills in strategic planning.

WORK EXPERIENCE

Assistant Director, Missouri Department of Education, Division of Library Development and Services, Jefferson City, MO 2001–present

- Facilitated the development and evaluation of MELNET, Missouri's Online Information Network.
- Consulted with libraries and state and local agencies on technology solutions for resource sharing.
- Served as state coordinator and liaison to public library directors.
- Provided access for over 30 new online resources in 2004.
- Served on Department of Education Digital Strategic Planning Committee and assisted in writing a plan.
- Extensive Web site design and development experience.

Coordinator, Electronic Reference Services, University of Delaware, Newark, DE, 1998–2001

- Administered university Computer Assisted Research and Reference Services Division.
- Managed collection development and budgeting for electronic resources in all disciplines
- Supervised 10 librarians.
- Developed policies and procedures for the division.
- Served as liaison with faculty.

Librarian, Headquarters Library, Dupont, Inc., Wilmington, DE, 1997–1998

- Provided extensive reference services to headquarters and 4 corporate libraries.
- Responded to over 50 complex reference requests each day.
- Managed acquisitions and original cataloging for all corporate libraries.
- Maintained all library technology including internal staff Web site.
- Recommended and implemented hardware and software solutions.

(continued)

Figure 5-5 Sample Technology/Systems Librarian Resume: Kratz (*Continued*)

Steven R. Kratz
Page 2

EDUCATION

M.A. in Library Science, University of Missouri, Colombia, MO, 1995.

B.A. in Political Science, Lincoln University, Jefferson City, MO, 1993.

PUBLICATIONS

Frequent reviewer for *Government Information Quarterly*.

"Annual Review of Best New Web Resources," *Web World*, 8 (June 2004).

"International Online Information Meeting Review, " *Library Technology News*, March, 2003.

PRESENTATIONS

Coordinated one-day seminar: "Managing Technology in Public Libraries," Library Executive Leadership Institute, Colombia, MO, 2002.

"Stop the Madness: Print vs. Electronic Resources," panelist at program of Association for Library Collections and Technical Services, American Library Association, Annual Conference, 2001.

PROFESSIONAL INVOLVEMENT

Special Interest Group for Applications and Technology (SIGAT)
- Consistent Interface Committee, member, 2003–04.
- Library Information Technology Committee, cochair, 2001–02.

Missouri Library Association
- Treasurer, 2004–05. Streamlined accounting procedures and budget recommendation procedures.

American Association of University Men
- Diversity Task Force Chair, Delaware Chapter, 2003–present.

OUTSIDE ACTIVITIES

- Participate in running marathons and triathlons. Placed second in age group, "Run for the Cure" race, 2000.

- Costume Director, Little Theater of Wilmington, 1997–99.

Figure 5-6   Sample Technology/Systems Librarian Resume: DiNardo

JACK DINARDO

1655 Telegraph Road
Des Moines, IA 50315
Office: 515.222.2433
jdinardo@aol.com

OBJECTIVE

A senior technology position involving significant Web design and administration.

QUALIFICATIONS

- Excellent systems background in a library environment.
- Ability to lead multiple projects simultaneously.
- Experienced Web administrator and designer.
- Ability to successfully lead teams.

WORK EXPERIENCE

Digital Projects Coordinator
Iowa State Library, Des Moines, IA, 2003–present

- Managed all aspects of state library Web site.
- Served as project manager for redesigned Web site including supervision of contract staff.
- Approved financial disbursements in excess of $2 million.
- Conducted usability studies including heuristic overviews and cognitive through testing.
- Managed migration of legacy-based "Communications" database.

Systems Librarian
Locust County Public Library System, Iowa City, IA, 2000–2003

- Supervised administration of library system Web site.
- Led the 25-member Library Operation's Computer Support Coordinator Program.
- Oversaw technical evaluation team for LAN support contract (over $1 million).
- Completed successful data analysis of journal usage to support interlibrary loan and collection development policy.

Research Librarian
Coalition for Internet Education, New York, NY, 1999–2000

- Researched current issues related to the Internet and education.
- Developed marketing materials for librarians and educators.
- Worked closely with members on local issues and advocacy.

EDUCATION

M.L.S., University of Iowa, School of Library and Information Science, 1999

B.A., History, Florida State University, Tallahassee, FL, 1997

(continued)

Figure 5-6   Sample Technology/Systems Librarian Resume: DiNardo (*Continued*)

Jack DiNardo, Page 2

PRESENTATIONS

- "Designing Usable Web Sites," with Florence Cox. Presentation at EducatorsWeb meeting in Salt Lake City, UT, 2005.

- "Web Redesign: A Cautionary Tale," at Federal Library Caucus meeting, Washington, D.C., 2004.

PROFESSIONAL
ACTIVITIES

Member, American Library Association. Regularly attend annual meetings.

Member, Usability Professionals Association.

AWARDS

- Group Award for Staff Training, Iowa State Library, 2005.

- Certificate of Appreciation in Recognition of Contributions to Locust County Public Library System Diversity Council, 2002.

Figure 5-7 Sample Technology/Systems Librarian Resume: Delong

Deborah Delong

Home: 64 East Holly Dr., Eugene, OR 97400; 541-346-1010
Office: University of Oregon, Knight Library, Eugene, OR 97403; 541-346-7143

Objective: A position as head of systems in a large public or academic library.

Summary of Qualifications

- Extensive systems experience in libraries.
- Experience working and negotiating with technology vendors.
- Background in technology planning and implementation.
- Experienced in all areas of administration including budget and staff training.

Professional Experience

Assistant Head of Systems, University of Oregon, Knight Library, Eugene, OR, 1995–present

- Assisted with planning, installation, and implementation of an online catalog system.
- Resolved all equipment and software problems.
- Performed a system analysis study on gift acquisitions and bindery functions.
- Oversaw the testing, certification, and installation of a new hardware and software for a LAN.
- Designed, implemented, and taught the staff training program for a new online catalog.
- Assisted in the supervision of 6 systems staff.

Acting Budget Officer, University of Oregon, Knight Library, 2000–01 (six months)

- Administered and managed a $5.6 million budget.
- Automated internal budget processing and developed new budgeting model.

American Library Association International Library Fellow, National Library, Estonia, 1998–99 (six months)

- Advised on technology for the country's public library system.
- Helped develop a five year automation plan.
- Advised on the selection of MARC record creation hardware and software and Novell network.
- Introduced the Internet including E-mail, gophers and Web.

Library System Intern, University of Washington, Seattle, WA, 1997-98

- Assisted with the development of a staff and user training program for the new online catalog system.
- Performed OCLC data entry.
- Assisted with Dialog searches and PC software training in the Graduate School's PC Lab.

(continued)

Figure 5-7   Sample Technology/Systems Librarian Resume: Delong (*Continued*)

Deborah Delong, Page 2

Education

M.L.I.S., University of Washington, Seattle, WA, 1998

B.S., Physics, Whitman College, Walla Walla, WA, 1996

Continuing Education: Earned 12 credits in University of North Dakota M.P.A. program, 2000; courses included statistics, research methodology, ethics, and organizational theory.

Honors

- Recipient, 3M/New Members Round Table Professional Development Grant, 1998.
- Beta Phi Mu (Library of Science Honorary Society), University of Washington, 1997.
- Alumni Scholarship, University of Washington, The Information School, 1997.

Selected Presentations

- Keynote address to the Library Association of Estonia, 1998.
- "Your Guide to the Web," presented at University of Oregon Library Conference, August 2002.
- "Library Networking in the 90's," a paper presented at the Oregon Council of Higher Education Computer Services Conference, 2001.

Selected Publications

- Numerous book reviews for *Information Technology in Libraries* and *Library Journal.*
- Editor, Newsletter, Oregon Library Association, 2003–present.
- "Online Resources in North Dakota's Libraries," a series of four articles published in the *Oregon Library Association Newsletter*, 2004.

Professional Activities

- President, Washington Student Chapter of the American Society of Information Science, 2004.
- Chair, Oregon Library Association Local Arrangements Committee, 2003 Annual Conference.
- Chair, Oregon Consortium of Academic Libraries, Technology Task Force, 2001 to present.

Figure 5-8 Sample Technology/Systems Librarian Resume: Kelly

Alice Fay Kelly

75 Swan Way
Fort Richmond, WA 98117
206.545.2930
EMAIL: kelly@yahoo.com

Objective: A position in a major corporate library with emphasis on product research and development.

Qualifications

- Administrative experience in a fast-paced corporate environment.
- Extensive knowledge of consumer online searching techniques.
- Excellent writer with emphasis on policy writing.
- Strong ability to lead teams and deliver products on time.

Work Summary

Book Program Manager
BooksOnline.com, 6470 Industrial Park S., Tacoma, WA, 2000–present

- Oversaw the browse (subject) category of major online bookseller.
- Collaborated with 8 editors to create more intuitive and relevant search terms.
- Hired twelve people within four weeks to staff music artist authority project.
- Developed communication plan to keep managers informed of project progress.
- Consulted closely with outside vendors on contracts.

Head of Reference and Information Services
Middlesex Regional Library, Bremerton, WA, 1999–2000

- Supervised twelve librarians.
- Oversaw all aspects of public service.
- Developed and implemented major policies for the library system.
- Chaired Networked Information Team which made major improvements in library technology.

Head, Circulation Division
Robert Crown Law Library, Stanford University, Palo Alto, CA, 1998–99

- Developed procedures for new Innovative Interfaces computer system.
- Designed and implemented a training program for library school interns and student workers.
- Developed a loan policy involving close consultation with faculty.
- Oversaw the development of an online test database to allow students to review former exams.

Education
- M.S., Library Science, Drexel University, Philadelphia, PA, 1999.
- M.B.A., The American University, Washington, DC, 1997.
- B.S., Physics, University of Wisconsin, Madison, 1986.

(continued)

Figure 5-8   Sample Technology/Systems Librarian Resume: Kelly (*Continued*)

Alice Fay Kelly, Page 2

Presentations

- American Association of Law Librarians, 94th Annual Meeting, "Subject Searching: Complexities for Law Librarians." Sole presenter for this national library conference, San Antonio, TX, 2003.
- Colorado Library Association, Annual Conference. "E-Commerce: Lessons for Libraries." Presented in Denver, CO, 2002.
- New England Library and Information Network (NELINT), Annual Meeting, "Catalogs in the 21st Century." Presented as part of a daylong program, Worchester, MA, 2002.
- American Association for Community Colleges, 84th Annual Conference, "Technology Skills for Student Success." One of four panelists, Urbana, IL, 2001.
- Frankfurt Book Fair, presentation at Collection Development Conference. Made two presentations on what libraries can learn from e-commerce, April 2000.
- California State Library, Internet Training Program, California Interactive Television. Participated in two-hour televised, interactive training workshop. Televised from Berkeley, CA, January 2000.

Publications

- "Prime Players in the Corporate Sector," *American Libraries*, March 2004, pp. 25–28.
- "BooksOnline.com Librarian Says Data Can Become Marketing Tool," *Business Journal Online*, Sept. 21, 2003. Interview by Harold Taylor.
- "Career Alternatives, "How to Expand Your Library Skills," *Drexel College of Information and Technology Quarterly*, Dec., 2002.

Professional Activities

American Library Association
- Member, Library Instruction Round Table, 2005. Cochair of annual conference program: "Library Instruction in Public Libraries."
- Chair, Machine-Readable Reference Services Section's Committee on Local Systems and Services, 2004.
- Washington Library Association, President, 2003–04. President of this 4,000-member organization.

Volunteer Experience

Board President, World Corps

- Serving second year 2 year term, 2005–06.
- Led non-profit that places Internet kiosks in rural developing nations.
- Set priorities and developed budget.

6 SAMPLE RESUMES: NONSUPERVISORY LIBRARIAN

TIPS FOR THE SAVVY RESUME WRITER

- If the employer wants subject expertise offer your qualification bullets or highlights in the work summary.
- Don't simply list the range of systems you have used or cite any specialized databases expertise.
- If the employer wants reference expertise, emphasize oral communication skills. Employers are always looking for candidates who can interact well with a variety of people.

MEET THE CANDIDATES

Christopher B. Gilpin is applying for a position as an earth sciences librarian. Note how carefully he has written his one-liner statements; all reinforce his job objective (see Figure 6-1). He also emphasized his subject expertise in the qualifications section.

Jason F. Gaynor's goal is to be a cataloger. His work experience is directly relevant to his targeted position, so he chooses a chronological format (see Figure 6-2).

Claudia Garcia is seeking a position as an assistant librarian/science reference librarian in a university library. The announcement for this position specifically states that the job requires an academic degree or extensive experience in science; demonstrated knowledge of electronic information resources; and excellent oral and written communication skills. Since Claudia has good experience in each of these areas, she chooses a functional format and tailors those headings to demonstrate her skill areas (see Figure 6-3). Her work history is not extensive, so she includes a nonprofessional position—the stamina required for the reference desk is not unlike that needed for waiting tables.

Susan Bradfield is seeking a position as a government information data librarian in a public library system. Note that Susan's resume is only one page; she is focused and delivers an excellent presentation that can be quickly read (see Figure 6-4). She effectively cites her professional activities in the qualifications section.

Figure 6-1   Sample Nonsupervisory Librarian Resume: Gilpin

Christopher B. Gilpin
1220 Old Concord Rd.
Boston, MA 02467
617.554.2422
E-MAIL: cbgilpin@yahoo.com

Objective: To work as Librarian (Earth Sciences) in the Blue Hill Meteorological Observatory Library, Harvard University.

Qualifications
- Extensive background in science librarianship.
- Experienced in working in fast-paced academic library.
- Broad knowledge of science databases.
- Ability to easily juggle multiple demands.
- Graduate degree in geology.

Work Summary

User Education/Reference Librarian & Earth Sciences Bibliographer
Catherine O'Connor Library at Weston Observatory, Boston College, Weston, MA, 2000–present
- Coordinated all user education activities.
- Selected, trained, and supervised student assistants.
- Scheduled reference desk and user education classes.
- Consulted with faculty on earth sciences sources and online services.
- Provided general reference in Science Library.

Librarian
Information Center, MEF Corporation, Newton, MA, 1999–2000
- Provided reference service to staff of 50 scientists.
- Performed searches using a variety of databases with particular emphasis on life sciences.
- Provided troubleshooting for computers.
- Compiled current awareness bibliographies for scientists.

Library Intern
Library, Long Island University, Brookville, NY, 1998–99
- Gave library tours to new students and faculty.
- Performed OCLC data entry.
- Provided reference service and completed database searches.

Education
- M.S., Library Science, Long Island University, Brookville, NY, 1999.
- M.A., Geology, University at Albany, State University of New York, 1997.
- B.S., Science, St. John's University, Jamaica, NY, 1986.

Publications
- *Science Libraries: Focus on Technology*, Occasional Paper #6, Special Libraries Association, 2003.

(continued)

Figure 6-1   Sample Nonsupervisory Librarian Resume: Gilpin (*Continued*)

Christopher B. Gilpin, Page 2

Professional Activities

Special Libraries Association
- Chair-Elect, Earth Sciences Division, 2005–06.

American Library Association
- Member, Association of College and Research Libraries, Forum on Science and Technology Library Research, 2002–03.

Figure 6-2   Sample Nonsupervisory Librarian Resume: Gaynor

Jason F. Gaynor

26 E. Williams Ave. #B-3
Ann Arbor, MI 48102
Office: 734.222.9456
jfgaynor@metro.com

OBJECTIVE: To work as a Cataloger.

HIGHLIGHTS OF QUALIFICATIONS

- Excellent knowledge of cataloging principles and procedures including AACR2.
- Experience in training staff in cataloging procedures.
- Working knowledge of French and Spanish.
- Experience with print and non-print formats.

WORK EXPERIENCE

Serials/GPO Records Librarian, Shapiro Undergraduate Library, University of Michigan, Ann Arbor, 2003–present

- Planned and directed acquisition, control, and cataloging of serials.
- Served as Superintendent of Documents (SuDocs) liaison.
- Maintained bibliographic, holdings, control, and retention records for U.S. government publications.
- Trained staff in technical services unit.
- Expert knowledge of AACR2, MARC, LCSH, LCCS and SuDocs classification and depository requirements.

Catalog Clerk, Library, Wayne State University, Detroit, MI, 2001–02

- Assisted in original cataloging, classification, and authority work for materials in all formats.
- Assisted with OCLC Enhance programs.
- Completed preparatory cataloging for French and Spanish materials.
- Received Superior Performance rating.

EDUCATION

M.L.I.S., Wayne State University, Detroit, MI, 2000.

B.A., Spanish, University of Puerto Rico, San Juan, PR, 1998. Graduate Cum laude.

LANGUAGES

Fluent in Spanish and French. Reading ability in German and Portuguese. Studied in Barcelona for three months while working on B.A.

(continued)

Figure 6-2 Sample Nonsupervisory Librarian Resume: Gaynor (*Continued*)

Jason F. Gaynor, Page 2

PROFESSIONAL AND OUTSIDE ACTIVITIES

Association for Library Collections & Technical Services (American Library Association)

- Member, Digital Resources Committee, 2001–02. Helping to plan President's program for annual conference: *Digital Resources: Planning for the Future.*

Special Libraries Association

- Member, Affirmative Action Committee, 2002–03.

Figure 6-3   Sample Nonsupervisory Librarian Resume: Garcia

CLAUDIA GARCIA
164 E. Quincy Drive
Blacksburg, VA 24061
Home: 540.421.1870 Office: 540.661.4310
cgarcia@telenet.com

OBJECTIVE	Assistant Librarian/Science Reference Librarian, University of Alabama.
QUALIFICATIONS	Reference experience with extensive science background. Proven writing and speaking abilities. Experienced searcher with electronic information resources. Ability to juggle multiple demands in high pressure environment.
EXPERIENCE	Science Reference • Provided in-person and telephone reference to students and faculty. • Knowledge of wide range of science sources. • Prepared bibliographies for faculty for curriculum development. • Evaluated science reference sources for professional recognition. Electronic Information Sources • Routinely used databases related to science reference including MEDLINE. • Experienced Web searcher. • Assisted in database budget planning. • Evaluated a wide range of electronic sources for possible acquisition. Writing and Speaking • Wrote circulation procedures manual. • Conducted classes for students on use of electronic resources. • Gave tours of library to visitors.
WORK HISTORY	2002–present Reference Librarian, Main Library, Virginia Tech, Blacksburg, VA 2001–02 Circulation Clerk, National Library of Medicine, Bethesda, MD 2000–01 Waitress (part-time), Tail of the Gator Bar & Grill, Tallahassee, FL
EDUCATION	Master of Science, School of Information Studies, Florida State University, Tallahassee, FL, 2000. Bachelor of Science in Physics, Barnard College, New York, NY, 1998.
PROFESSIONAL INVOLVEMENT	Special Libraries Association • Bulletin Editor, Science and Technology Division, 2003–04. Created popular column called "Science Reference Exchange." • Membership Committee, Nuclear Science Division, 2002–03.
OTHER ACTIVITIES	Sports: Tennis, swimming, biking. National High School Chess Association: Coach students on competitive play and serve as judge in contests.

Figure 6-4 Sample Nonsupervisory Librarian Resume: Bradfield

Susan Bradfield

2941 E. Rosemont Ave.
Iowa City, IA 52242
Office: 319.232.5455
Bradfield@conga.net

OBJECTIVE

Government Information Data Librarian, Birmingham Public Library.

QUALIFICATIONS

- Wide range of experience in delivering government data.
- Extensive database searching skills.
- Entire library career devoted to providing technical data to a variety of clients.
- Active professional involvement in activities related to delivery of government information.

WORK EXPERIENCE

Technical Information Specialist, Iowa Department of Transportation, Iowa City, IA, 2002–present
- Maintained library for state agency which provides data to other state agencies and local governments.
- Used a wide range of software packages to deliver statistical information.
- Provided computer support to library and statistical units.
- Compiled annual report of Iowa transportation statistics.

Economics Librarian, Marvin A. Pomerantz Business Library, University of Iowa, Iowa City, IA, 2000–02
- Provided business and economic reference to students and faculty.
- Searched on many different databases related to economics.
- Served as liaison to Economics Department.
- Developed and implemented orientation sessions for new Economics Department students.

Library Assistant, Iowa Bibliographic Council, Inc., Dallas, TX, 1999–2000
- Assisted in the development of training materials.
- Provided telephone reference and troubleshooting assistance.
- Knowledge of cataloging rules, MARC formats, and OCLC online systems.

EDUCATION

Master of Library and Information Science, University of Iowa, Iowa City, IA, 1999.

Bachelor of Arts, Economics, University of Idaho, Moscow, ID, 1997.

PROFESSIONAL ACTIVITIES

Special Libraries Association
- Chair, Transportation Section, 2004–05. Coordinated publication of SLA bibliography on transportation sources.
- Chair, Government Documents Section, 2003.

Iowa Library Association
- Member, Networking Committee, 2000–01.

7 SAMPLE RESUMES: SUPERVISORY/ MANAGEMENT LIBRARIAN

TIPS FOR THE SAVVY RESUME WRITER

- Clearly identify your accomplishments to demonstrate that you are results oriented. How have you improved service, streamlined operations, saved money, or implemented a system that solved problems?
- Add any relevant leadership activities you may have performed on an ad hoc basis. Think of the times that were beyond routine management duties. Have you led a committee? What did the committee produce? Did you write a report? Were the recommendations implemented? What were the results?
- Did you receive temporary promotions or acting positions?
- Remember to include leadership activities in professional or volunteer positions.

MEET THE CANDIDATES

Edward T. Chase is applying for a position as manager of technical services at a large university. His experience is excellent and he chooses the chronological format to highlight his relevant qualifications in his current position (see Figure 7-1).

Olivia A. Henderson is a media coordinator in a medium-size school district and seeks a progressively more responsible position in a larger system. Note her "Educational Philosophy" statement; this is slightly unconventional, but works well with her background and job objective (see Figure 7-2).

Amal Batale is currently head of reference at a large academic library. His current job objective is to obtain a position as an associate dean for a small or mid-size university library. Because James has had progressively more responsible positions in one academic library and he wants to capitalize on the prestige of this institution, he chooses the chronological format (see Figure 7-3). Note how well he has quantified his accomplishments (number of students taught, number of staff supervised, etc.).

Wendy G. Castleton is a library science professor with a specialty in school library media. She has extensive teaching experience and has published widely. Her resume is a Curriculum Vitae—it contains comprehensive information on her speaking, publishing, and research activities (see Figure 7-4). The CV is generally used for academic positions. Note that Wendy has not given a detailed description of all her positions; rather she has included positions from the last four years. Older positions are indicated in summary form. To emphasize her distinguished academic achievements, she has moved the "Education" section above the "Work Experience."

Jessica Brighton is access services head in a large university. Her goal is to find a position as director of public services in a medium or large-size university. Note how well she uses the combination resume to highlight her important skill areas (see Figure 7-5).

Terry Wong is currently head of public services in a major university library, and his career has steadily progressed in this institution. He now seeks a position with more responsibility and is applying for the head of a university science and technology library. Because he has been with one institution for a long time, he chooses the combination resume style to emphasize the broad range of skills he has acquired in several positions (see Figure 7-6).

Jeremy R. Fisher is currently a branch manager in a large public library system. He would like to secure a position as assistant director of a small to medium-size public library, and has employed the chronological format to showcase his excellent job progression (see Figure 7-7).

Figure 7-1   Sample Supervisory Librarian Resume: Chase

Edward T. Chase
Elizabethtown College Library
Elizabethtown, PA 17072-2298
717.421.9783   etc@verizon.net

Objective: A position as Manager of Technical Services with Auburn University Library.

QUALIFICATIONS

- Supervisory and administrative experience in a technologically complex library environment.
- State-of-the-art knowledge of serial technology.
- Strong background in acquisitions, cataloging, and processing.
- Experience in a university environment.

WORK EXPERIENCE

Supervisor, Cataloging and Systems Department, 2001–present
Elizabethtown College Library, Elizabethtown, PA

- Administered all cataloging and systems activities of the library and supervised 15 staff members in this department.
- Experienced with MARC, DDC, AACR2, OCLC, LC subject headings, and authority control.
- Coordinated use of NOTIS and all library network activities.
- Streamlined cataloging operation which reduced processing time by one week.
- Serve as liaison to the Pennsylvania Consortium of College Libraries.

Product and Customer Service Manager, 1999–2001
Moomaw Library Services, Dayton, VA

- Planned and designed serials and acquisitions components of integrated library automation system.
- Coordinated user group newsletter and forums at national conferences.
- Demonstrated systems to libraries on a routine basis.
- Honored with "Product Manager of the Year" award for consistently high performance.

Head of Serials, 1997–99
University of Chicago, Graduate Library, Chicago, IL

- Supervised all serials activities including cataloging, claiming, check-in, binding, and replacement.
- Oversaw ongoing reclassification.
- Planned and implemented transition to automated serials system.
- Headed updating of University of Chicago Library Consortium Union List of Serials.

(continued)

Figure 7-1   Sample Supervisory Librarian Resume: Chase (*Continued*)

Edward T. Chase, Page 2

Serials Cataloger, 1996–97
Florida Southern College, Lakeland, FL 33102

- Performed and revised all serials cataloging.
- Established and maintained series authority file.
- Processed continuations and checked in nonperiodical series using OCLC serials control subsystem.
- Cataloged microfilms, music scores, and monographs in areas of music and literature.

EDUCATION

M.L.I.S., University of British Columbia, Vancouver, BC, Canada, 1995.

M.A., History, University of Pittsburgh, Pittsburgh, PA, 1993.

B.A., English Literature, Hamilton College, Clinton, NY, 1989.

PROFESSIONAL MEMBERSHIP AND ACTIVITIES

American Library Association

Association for Library Collections & Technical Services
- Chair, Serials Section Committee to Study Serials Standards, 2003–04.
- Chair, Serials Section Union Lists of Serials Committee, 2002–03.

Association of College and Research Libraries
- Standards and Accreditation Committee, 2004–05.
- Academic Status Committee, 1998–99.

Pennsylvania Library Association
- Chair, Library Technology Subgroup, 2002–03. Planned and implemented a major program on networking at the 2003 annual conference.

North American Serials Interest Group

- Electronic Communications Committee, 2003–04.

PRESENTATIONS

- Workshop Presenter, "Union Lists: A Sheep in Wolf's Clothing?" at North American Serials Interest Group, 2004.
- ACRL Mid-Atlantic Serials Group presentation, "Standards That Will Change Your World," Sept. 2004.
- Presenter, Computers in Libraries Conference, "Acquisitions: Don't Look Back!," June, 2003.

Figure 7-2 Sample Supervisory Librarian Resume: Henderson

OLIVIA A. HENDERSON

1612 Edgefield Rd. • Salt Lake City, UT 84121 • Office: 208-243-6541
Home: 208-594-3334 • E-mail: oahenderson@aol.com

Objective: To serve as Library Media Services Director, Cliff County Schools, Buffalo, NY.

Educational Philosophy

Students deserve the opportunities to use their unique talents and abilities in their quest for learning. The library media program provides materials, instruction, and curriculum integration to maximize learning situations to meet the needs of staff and students. Lifelong learners become literate, contributing members of society.

Qualifications

- Broad-based experience in all areas of library media coordination and development.
- Extensive technology skills, including online circulation/cataloging and networking.
- Strong interpersonal skills in working with students, teachers, and parents.
- Successful manager of Instructional Media Center.

Experience

District Library Media Coordinator and Library Media Director, Greater Salt Lake City, Salt Lake City, UT, 2000–present

- Coordinated library media services including community outreach, technology integration, policies and procedures, curriculum, strategic planning, and facilities.
- Involved in all areas of planning for two new libraries at the intermediate and middle school level.
- Directed elementary library media center including acquisitions, technology, reading enrichment programs, and supervision of staff and volunteers.
- Represented school district on wide range of committees.

Salt Lake City Summer EXCEL Director, Summers 1998–2000

- Planned and directed the summer school program, grades pre-K through 12.
- Devised budget, hired four staff members, and coordinated course offerings and support services.
- Supervised daily operation of the program.

(continued)

Figure 7-2   Sample Supervisory Librarian Resume: Henderson (*Continued*)

Olivia A. Henderson, Page 2

Library Media Specialist (K–5 and 6–8 grades), Bath County Schools, Bath, VA, 1994–98

- Developed training program for computers and new library research skills curriculum.
- Acquired funding for materials through *Staunton News Leader* grants, book fairs, and private donations.
- Reallocated elementary library space, creating a story corner with puppet theater and computer lab.
- Managed computer hardware/software use including maintenance and purchases.
- Developed library skills curriculum and literature appreciation activities.
- Coordinated first system telelecture.
- Implemented reading enrichment programs through Book Clubs and annual read-in/sleep-over activities.
- Opened new middle school library with automated catalog and circulation.

Additional Work Experience

1997–98	Document Specialist	Accel Computers, Inc., Waynesboro, VA
1995–97	Reference Librarian	Mary Baldwin College, Staunton, VA
1994–95	Graduate Assistant	Clark Atlanta University, Atlanta, GA
1992–94	English Teacher	Atlanta Public School System, Atlanta, GA

Education

Master of Science in Library Science, University of Southern Mississippi, School of Library and Information Science, Hattiesburg, MS, 1995.

Bachelor of Science in chemistry, University of Mississippi, Oxford, MS, 1992.

Certificates and Licenses

Utah licenses

- Supervisor/Coordinator/Director of Instruction
- Instructional Library Media Specialist
- Instructional Technology Specialist
- Principal
- Secondary English

Honors and Awards

- Dane County Cultural Commission Grant Recipient, 2005.
- Chrysler Family Reading Grant Recipient, 2004.
- Finalist for American Association of School Librarians, National School Library Media Program of the Year Award, 2003.
- *Staunton News Leader* Educators Grant Recipient: 1994, 1995, 1998.
- 3M/JMRT (Junior Members Round Table now, New Members Round Table), American Library Association, Professional Grant Recipient, 1995.

(continued)

Figure 7-2 Sample Supervisory Librarian Resume: Henderson (*Continued*)

Olivia A. Henderson, Page 3

Professional Association Activities

American Library Association
- Councilor, elected at-large, 2002–05.
- Council Caucus Chair, 2001–02. Led meeting of Council members to review issues.
- Junior Members Round Table
    Chair, Olofson Grant Committee, 1997–98.
    Chair, Committee on Governance, 1997–98.
    Director of Publications, 1995–96.
- American Association of School Librarians
    Chair, Microcomputers in the Schools Award Committee, 1999–2000.
    Member, Long-Range Planning Committee, 1997–98.
- Library Administration and Management Association
    Member, Staff Development Committee, 2003–04.
- Utah Educational Media Association
    Member, Awards Committee, 2000–01.
    School Restructuring Ad-Hoc Committee, 2003.

Presentations

- "Catch a Caldecott" and "Picture Books and Beyond"–Fay Kaigler Children's Literature Conference, University of Southern Mississippi, Hattiesburg, MS, 2004.

Publications

- Regular columnist for *Library Talk*, 1997–98.
- "A Library Skills Curriculum for Elementary School Students," *Library Talk*, April, 1996.
- Coeditor for new journal in development, *HITS: Helping Integrate Topics in Schools*.

Community Involvement

- Salt Lake City Public Library Board, 2000–present.
- Girl Scout Leader, 2000–present.
- Bath County Cable Commission, 1995–97.

Figure 7-3 Sample Supervisory Librarian Resume: Batale

Amal Batale

1440 Mountain View Way • Ft. Collins, CO 80523
Office: 970.412.8381 • E-mail: amal@earthlink.com

OBJECTIVE: Associate Dean in a small or medium-size academic library.

SUMMARY OF QUALIFICATIONS

- Successfully administered complex reference activities in large university library.
- Developed innovative user instruction courses.
- Extensive background in collection development administration.
- Reputation for strong commitment to improving service for library patrons.

WORK HISTORY

Undergraduate Library, Colorado State University, Ft. Collins, CO

Head of Reference
2001 to present
- Coordinated all Reference Department activities including Database Services, Government Documents, Bibliographic Instruction, and Outreach.
- Supervised 11 full-time and 5 part-time staff.
- Recruited, hired, and trained all reference staff.
- Planned and implemented all staff development activities.
- Developed library instruction class which combined online tutorials available through campus network with traditional tours.
- Coordinated all reference collection development.

History Reference Librarian and Outreach Coordinator
1997 to 2001
- Recommended books and periodicals for reference collection.
- Provided reference assistance to faculty, staff, and students.
- Instructed hundreds of students each semester on how to use the library.
- Taught "Introduction to Reference" in School of Library and Information Science.
- Implemented special library tours for local elementary schools.
- Served as Acting Bibliographic Instruction Coordinator, 1988.
- Supervised and wrote evaluations for reference interns.

University Archives, University of California at Berkeley, Berkeley, CA

Archives Technician
1996
- Reorganized student record microfilm collection.
- Designed online system for tracking microfilm loans.
- Designed more efficient shelving arrangement for collection.
- Wrote "Finding Guide to University Archives Microfilm."

(continued)

Figure 7-3 Sample Supervisory Librarian Resume: Batale (*Continued*)

Amal Batale   Page 2

EDUCATION

M.L.S., School of Information, University of Michigan, Ann Arbor, MI, 1995.

A.B.D., in History, University of Washington, Seattle.

Certificate in Archival Training, Columbia University, New York, NY, 1994.

M.A., History, Syracuse University, Syracuse, NY, 1993.

B.A., French and History, Syracuse University, Syracuse, NY, 1990.

PROFESSIONAL ACTIVITIES

American Library Association
- Chair, Diversity Committee, Association of College and Research Libraries, 2004 to 2005.
- Coordinator, Discussion Group—"Performance Issues for Reference/Information Librarians," Reference and Adult Services Division, 2003.

Organization of American Historians
- Member, Nominating Committee, 2005.
- Member, Archival Standards Committee, 2000 to 2001.
  - Co-authored "Archival Standards: A Review of the Past Decade," 2001.

OTHER ACTIVITIES

National Cystic Fibrosis Society
- Cochaired 10K Run which raised over $ 40,000 in contributions.

Other interests include running, photography, paleontology, nature, conservation, drawing, and music.

Figure 7-4 Sample Supervisory Librarian Resume: Castleton

CURRICULUM VITAE
WENDY G. CASTLETON
University of Texas
School of Information
Sanchez Building
1 University Station
Austin, TX 78712-0390
512.333.2425 EMAIL: wgc@aol.com

OBJECTIVE: Dean of a school of library and information science.

HIGHLIGHTS OF QUALIFICATIONS

- Ten years of teaching experience at university level.
- Ph.D. in library and information science.
- Recognized authority on school library media programs.
- Author of numerous articles on all aspects of librarianship.

EDUCATION

University of Maryland	Ph.D.	Library and Information Science, 2002
University of Pittsburgh	M.S.	Computer Education and Cognitive Systems, 2001
University of Pittsburgh	M.L.S.	Specialization: School Libraries, 1990
Sarah Lawrence College	B.A.	English and Education, 1987

WORK EXPERIENCE

Assistant Professor, School Library Media Program, University of Texas, School of Information, Austin, TX, 2003 to present
- Taught in children's services and literature, computer applications for libraries, information technologies, school libraries, and information ethics.
- Extensive research in the following areas:
    Innovation diffusion and technology integration in school library media centers and graduate library education.
    Impact of school library media centers on academic achievement.
    Communication channels of school library media specialists.

School of Library and Information Studies, University of Oklahoma, Tulsa, OK

Adjunct Professor/Doctoral Research Associate, 2001–02
- Taught courses in children's and young adult literature.
- Provided online and research services for the faculty of the University's Oklahoma Center for Educational Technology (OCET).
- Taught bibliographic instruction for OCET workshops and classes.

Director, Information Retrieval Laboratory/Doctoral Teaching Associate, 1998–02
- Taught courses in media production and services, local area networks, computers for libraries, and children's literature.
- Supervised all Laboratory operations and Master's level student lab assistants.
- Conducted bibliographic instruction and class demonstrations of Web, including OCLC.

(continued)

Figure 7-4   Sample Supervisory Librarian Resume: Castleton (*Continued*)

Castleton, Page 2

ADDITIONAL WORK HISTORY

1995-98   Elementary Library Media Specialist, King George County Schools, Bronxville, NY
1994-95   High School Librarian, Troy County Public Schools, Troy, NY
1993   Government Documents/Reference Librarian, Long Island Library District, Montauk, NY

CURRENT RESEARCH

"Education and Training Needs of Information Professionals in Public Libraries for Virtual Reference Services," in progress.

"The Impact of School Library Media Centers in Texas on Academic Achievement." Sponsored by the School Library Media Section of the Texas Library Association, 2003-04.

ARTICLES

"The Future is Now: Revamping Virtual Reference Service Education for School Library Media Specialists and Youth Services Librarians." In *Proceedings of the 2004 Virtual Reference Desk Conference*, 2005, in press.

"School Libraries in the United States of America, An Update Report," *School Libraries Worldwide: The Journal of the International Association of School Libraries*, July 2002.

"Attitudes of School Library Media Specialists Toward Networking," *School Library Media Quarterly*, Summer, 2001.

"Credentialing of Online Database Searchers," co-authored with Ralph Brite, *LIBRES: Library and Information Science Research Electronic Journal*, No. 3, October, 2000.

Frequent contributor and book/software reviewer to:
* School Library Journal
* Emergency Librarian
* Library Journal

Children's book reviewer/previewer for Harcourt Brace, HarperCollins, and Scholastic.

Manuscript referee for *School Library Media Quarterly*, *School Libraries Worldwide*, and *Emergency Librarian*.

PAPER AND PROGRAM PRESENTATIONS

"It's Not Just a Matter of Ethics 2: An Examination of the Issues Related to the Ethical Provision of Consumer Health Services in Public Libraries." In *Ethics of Electronic Information*. This paper was presented at the Ethics of Electronic Information Conference, Memphis, 2003.

"Electronic Resources for School Library Media Specialists," research program presented at the Association of Library and Information Science Educators (ALISE), National Conference, Salt Lake City, UT, February, 2002.

"School Library Media Centers and Impact on Academic Achievement," program presented at the American Association of School Librarians (AASL) National Conference, Cleveland, OH, October, 2001.

"Recent Trends in Children's Literature," program presented to the Reading Teachers Association of Western Oklahoma, May, 2000.

(continued)

Figure 7-4 Sample Supervisory Librarian Resume: Castleton (*Continued*)

Castleton, Page 3

"The Role of the School Library in Library Networks," paper presented at New York Library Association, Albany, NY, 1999.

Numerous workshops and institutes for school districts and local conferences, particularly on computer applications for libraries and technology integration into curriculum.

GRANTS

Association for Library and Information Science Education (ALISE)/Online Computer Library Association (OCLC) Research Grant Award, $15,000.

U. S. Department of Education, Title IIB of the Higher Education Act, Library Training for School Library Media Specialist, 2003-04. Grant for $20,000.

Oklahoma Library Association Research Grant, 2000-02. Grant for $5,500. For research on "The Impact of School Library Media Centers in Pennsylvania on Academic Achievement."

PROFESSIONAL ASSOCIATION ACTIVITIES

AMERICAN LIBRARY ASSOCIATION

    American Association of School Librarians (AASL)
        AASL President, 2004-05.
        Restructuring Taskforce, 2004-05.
        Research Committee, 2002-03; Chair, 2003-04.
        Highsmith Research Award Committee, 2002-03.
        Lance Study Replication Committee, 2002-03.
        Membership Committee, 1986-89; Chair, 2001-02.
        Microcomputers in the School Library Award Committee, Chair, 2000-01.
        School Library Media Program of the Year Award Committee, 1999-2000.

    Association for Library Services to Children
        Boy Scouts of America Advisory Committee, 2001-03, Chair, 2003-06.

    Library Administration and Management Association
        BES-School Libraries Facility Committee, 2001-02.

    Young Adult Library Services Association
        Computer Applications Committee, 2001-03; Chair, 2003-04.

    Library Research Round Table
        Chair-Elect, 2004-05; Chair, 2005-06.
        Executive Board, Member-at-Large, 2004-05.

    International Association of School Librarians
        Editorial Board, IASL Journal, *School Libraries Worldwide*, 2004-07.

    Texas Library Association
        Continuing Education Committee, 2005-06.

    School Library Media Section
        Research Committee, 2005-07.
        Executive Board, 2004-05.

(continued)

Figure 7-4   Sample Supervisory Librarian Resume: Castleton (*Continued*)

Castleton, Page 4

HONORS AND AWARDS

- *Who's Who in America 2005.*
- Beta Phi Mu (National Library Science Honor Society), 1990.
- Phi Delta Kappa (National Education Fraternity), 1996.
- Presidential Academic Scholarship, Sarah Lawrence College, 1987.

INSTITUTIONAL AND COMMUNITY SERVICE

University of Texas, Austin
   Computing and Instructional Technology (CIT) Committee, 2004–present.
   Becker Hall Space Planning Task Force, 2003 to present.
   Curriculum Committee, 1993–96; Chair, 2003–04.

Parent Teacher Student Association (PTSA) Volunteer
   Educational Policy Committee, Central School District, 2003–04.
   American Educator Awards Committee, 1994-96; Chair, 2004–06.

Certified National U.S. Swimming Stroke & Turn Official.

Figure 7-5 Sample Supervisory Librarian Resume: Brighton

JESSICA BRIGHTON

University of Kentucky
Education Library
Lexington, KY 40506-0039
859-203-4589
brighton@mindspring.net

Objective: To serve as a director or head of public services for a large university.

SUMMARY OF QUALIFICATIONS

- Experience in all aspects of public services in an academic setting.
- Implemented new policies and procedures which improved customer service.
- Supervised staff in public services and security.
- Extensive background in Interlibrary Loan.

WORK EXPERIENCE

Access Services Department Head (1999–present) and
Assistant Professor of Bibliography (2002–present)
University of Kentucky Libraries, Education Library, Lexington, KY

Management and Administration
- Supervised, trained, and evaluated 8 Access Services staff.
- Administered department budget and submitted yearly plan.
- Managed all building security.
- Collected and analyzed a wide range of data for management and strategic planning.

Circulation
- Formulated and implemented a proposal for telephone notification of overdue materials.
- Created a Reserve customer satisfaction survey.
- Implemented a borrower's card policy which has resulted in income of over $10,000 to date.
- Trained personnel on circulation functions of NOTIS.
- Created a customer service satisfaction survey analysis for Interlibrary Loan.

Teaching
- Taught one course every semester. Courses included: Staff Development in Libraries; Introduction to Bibliography; and History of the Book.

ADDITIONAL WORK EXPERIENCE

Government Documents Librarian, University of Puerto Rico, San Juan, PR, 1998–99

Media Librarian, College of Education, Learning Resource Center, Yale University, New Haven, CT, 1997–98

(continued)

Figure 7-5   Sample Supervisory Librarian Resume: Brighton (*Continued*)

Jessica Brighton, Page 2

EDUCATION

M.L.I.S., University of Denver, Denver, CO, 1997.

B.S., Education Technology, Tufts University, Medford, MA, 1995.

PRESENTATIONS/WORKSHOPS

"University of Kentucky Web Resources," School of Library and Information Science, Lexington, KY, Jan., 2002.

"Accommodating Change Through Training," Association of College and Research Libraries Conference, Salt Lake City, UT, April, 2001.

"Training for Automated Circulation Systems," panel presenter, Annual Conference, Kentucky Library Association, 2000.

PUBLICATIONS

"The Future of Access Services," with Jane Terra, *Collection Management*, Jan., 2002, vol. 5, p. 12.

"Circulation Desk Operations," *College and Research Libraries News* 52, p. 994.

PROFESSIONAL ACTIVITIES

Kentucky Library Association
- Technology Round Table, Chair, 2003–04.
- Interlibrary Loan Cooperation Committee, 2002–03.

American Library Association
   Association of College and Research Libraries
- Chapters Council, 2004.

   Library Administration and Management Association
- Staff Development Committee—Coordinated major revision of *Staff Development: A Practical Guide*.

AWARDS

University of Kentucky Associates Distinguished Lectureship, 2004.

University of Kentucky Faculty Career Development Award, 2003.

Figure 7-6   Sample Supervisory Librarian Resume: Wong

TERRY WONG

2471 Wright Blvd. • Milwaukee, WI 53233
Office: 414.255.4329   tw@netzero.net

OBJECTIVE: To serve as Head of the Science and Technology Library, The University of Ohio.

SUMMARY OF QUALIFICATIONS

- Experienced public services administrator in a science library.
- Broad knowledge of collection development in the sciences.
- Extensive experience with searching electronic databases.
- Proven interpersonal skills with faculty, students, and staff.

WORK EXPERIENCE

Education and Science Library, Raymor Memorial Libraries, Marquette University, Marquette, WI

Head of Public Services, 2001–present

Administration
- Coordinated and supervised circulation, reference, and processing staff in all public service activities.
- Led team that planned move of over 45,000 volumes to off-site storage.
- Managed public services budget.

Technology
- Planned and implemented the Library's automated circulation system.
- Assisted in development of network.
- Evaluated science electronic services including full-text databases and Web resources.

Reference/Instruction Librarian and Psychology Specialist, 1998–01

Reference
- Provided in-person reference in the field of psychology.
- Worked closely with faculty to develop course bibliographies and reserve collections.
- Scheduled reference desk and user education activities.

Collection Development
- Served as liaison to the Psychology Department for collection development.
- Reviewed psychology literature and publishers' catalogs to select material for the collection.
- Monitored the psychology book and serials fund.
- Team member on Collection Review Committee which made decisions on weeding, storage, and journal selections.

(continued)

Figure 7-6 Sample Supervisory Librarian Resume: Wong (*Continued*)

Terry Wong, Page 2

TEACHING EXPERIENCE

Adjunct Faculty, University of Wisconsin, School of Library and Information Studies, Madison. Taught the following courses:
- Bibliography: Theory and Technique, 1995.
- Information Resources and Libraries, 1992–94.
- Seminar in Science and Technology Reference, 1995.

ADDITIONAL WORK EXPERIENCE

Psychology Bibliographer   1994–98   Education and Science Library, Raymor Memorial Libraries, Marquette University

Reference Intern   1992–93   Graduate Library, Boston College

EDUCATION

M.L.S., Simmons College, Graduate School of Library and Information Sciences, Boston, MA, 1993.

Ph.D., Experimental Psychology, New York University, New York, NY, 1991. Dissertation: *Spreading Cortical Depression in Mice.*

M.A., Experimental Psychology, New York University, New York, NY, 1987.

B.S., Psychology, Vassar College, Poughkeepsie, NY, 1985. Graduated Summa cum laude.

PUBLICATIONS

"Computer-Assisted Instruction: Is It an Option for Bibliographic Instruction in Large Undergraduate Survey Classes?" in *College and Research Libraries* 59, no. 1, January 2003: 19–27.

"The Psychology of Learning and Cognitive Styles—Practical Implications for Teaching," *Learning to Teach–Workshops on Instructions.* Edited by the Learning to Teach Task Force, Bibliographic Instruction Section, Association of College and Research Libraries, American Library Association, Chicago, 2003.

"Mentoring Science Students," *Special Libraries* 85, no. 4, Fall, 2002.

Frequent book review contributor to *Library Quarterly* and *Library Journal.*

Currently writing a book entitled *Emerging Technologies and the Library*, for Hayworth Press.

PRESENTATIONS

"Comparing Modes of Instruction," ACRL Bibliographic Instruction and Research Sections and Library Instruction Round Table program: "Improve Instruction Through Evaluation," Philadelphia, 2004. Also, facilitated group instruction.

"Developing a Library Instruction Program," New York Clearinghouse on Library Instruction Open House, Feb. 4, 2003.

(continued)

Figure 7-6 Sample Supervisory Librarian Resume: Wong (*Continued*)

Terry Wong, Page 3

RESEARCH AND GRANT ACTIVITIES

- ALA/ACRL Institute on Information Literacy Immersion Program—member of founding faculty responsible for developing curriculum for inaugural program and presenting instruction at first Immersion Program in 2000, Plattsburg, NY.

- Marquette University Office of Instruction Development Improvement Programs grant for development of a computer-assisted instruction program to teach undergraduate psychology students the organization of and access to journal material in the life sciences, 2003-04.

PROFESSIONAL ACTIVITIES

American Library Association

ALA Office of Accreditation—Site team member for External Accreditation Review for the University of Washington, 2004.

Association of College and Research Libraries—Bibliographic Instruction Section
    Learning to Teach Task Force, 2002-03.
    Education for Bibliographic Instruction Committee, 2001.

New Members Round Table
    Chair, Nominating Committee, 2000-01.
    Director for Membership, Awards and Continuing Education Committees, 1999-2000.
    EBSCO Scholarship Committee Chair, 1998-99.

Member: American Psychological Association, Medical Library Group of Massachusetts, Phi Beta Mu, Social and Behavioral Sciences Librarians Network.

Figure 7-7   Sample Supervisory Librarian Resume: Fisher

JEREMY R. FISHER
2424 Sunset Street
Bozeman, MT 59771-1230
Office: 612.513.2433
jrfisher@aol.com

OBJECTIVE

Assistant Director of a public library system

QUALIFICATIONS

- Significant supervisory and administrative experience in a large public library.
- Broad experience in managing branch libraries of different sizes.
- Excellent knowledge of all aspects of library technology and emerging technologies.
- Experience managing complex budgets and services.

WORK EXPERIENCE

Bozeman Public Library System, Bozeman, MT

Branch Manager, Sunnydale Branch, 2002–present

- Managed largest branch in library system (annual circulation exceeding one million).
- Proposed, designed, and implemented Division for the Visually Impaired.
- Served as chair of Public Library System Staff Development Committee.
- Supervised a diverse staff of 30 employees.
- Coordinated move and opening of 26,000-square-foot branch library.

Branch Manager, Fashion Galleria Mall Branch, 1999–2002

- Managed busy storefront branch in shopping mall.
- Designed and implemented library computer center.
- Applied for and received grant to have a mural painted in the library as part of the Art for Public Places Program.
- Coordinated a program for Latchkey Children which was nationally recognized in library press.
- Led book discussion groups on a monthly basis.

Head, Youth Services Department, Central Library, 1997–99

- Planned, directed, and implemented all library services for children.
- Supervised staff of 7.
- Implemented a wide range of electronic resources for children.
- Designed outreach activities including local school visits.
- Gained excellent knowledge of children's literature.

EDUCATION

M.L.S., University of Maryland, College of Library and Information Science, 1994

B.A., Political Science, Lynchburg College, Lynchburg, VA, 1992

(continued)

Figure 7-7   Sample Supervisory Librarian Resume: Fisher (*Continued*)

Jeremy R. Fisher, Page 2

PROFESSIONAL ACTIVITIES	Montana Library Association
	• Elected to several leadership positions including: President, 2003–04 and Treasurer, 2002–03.
	• Chair, Reference Interest Group, 2002.
	
	American Library Association
	    Young Adult Library Services Association
	  • Chair, YALSA Intellectual Freedom Committee, 2003.
	
	Represented Montana Library Association at ALA/Intellectual Freedom Committee Leadership Training Institute, 1999.

8 SAMPLE RESUMES: RECENT GRADUATES OF LIBRARY SCHOOL PROGRAMS

TIPS FOR THE SAVVY RESUME WRITER

- Writing a resume can be especially challenging for those just graduating from library school or just beginning their careers. Do not let the fact that you have virtually no professional experience reflect in your resume.
- Use the functional format if you don't have significant work experience.
- Employers look for potential. In your professional and volunteer experiences describe any leadership positions.
- Emphasize an M.L.S. degree by including it under the qualifications heading.
- Identify any courses you have completed in graduate school that are germane to the position.
- Don't be afraid to mention nonprofessional work experience. There are some skills in these positions that are transferable to professional positions.
- Be sure to include skills and accomplishments from other nonlibrary professional positions. Oral and written communication abilities can be particularly relevant.

MEET THE CANDIDATES

Audrey Newhouse is a recent library school graduate who has just completed a one-year position as a librarian with a government advisory commission that is going out of business. While her job search is focused on association and nonprofit organization libraries, she is also interested in newspaper libraries that might capitalize on her previous experience as a reporter. Since her professional library experience is somewhat limited, Audrey chooses a functional format for her resume to highlight the good range of skills she has acquired in library as well as nonlibrary positions (see Figure 8-1). Because she anticipates that her prospective employer may not have a library background, she has paid special attention to describing her experience in clear terms. Although she lacks professional association involvement, she has not forgotten relevant volunteer work.

Brandon G. Hazzard seeks a business reference librarian position in a university. Note how effectively he uses one-liners to support his job objective (see Figure 8-2). Also, his choice of the functional format helps showcase his most relevant skill area. Note especially that he has highlighted his extensive database skills by including this as a separate heading.

Alicia C. Bolanos is applying for a position as Librarian I/Bibliographer for the social sciences and journalism. The job posting stresses the following areas as most critical: subject expertise in journalism and the social sciences; skill in the use of print and electronic information sources in these fields; knowledge of a foreign language; and good oral and written communication skills. Alicia's resume reflects the thorough job she did completing her personal inventory—she references a number of useful professional and outside activities that support her qualifications for this position (see Figure 8-3).

Adam P. Hemingway is a applying for a position as a children's librarian in a public library. Although he doesn't have a great deal of experience, he has documented significant activities related to service for children. He has used a functional format to create a very effective one-page resume (see Figure 8-4).

Erica E. O'Neill completed her M.L.S. about a year ago and has had several good temporary positions. Her goal is a permanent position as a reference librarian, and Erica is applying for a specific job in an academic library. At first glance, it might appear that a functional format would be most advantageous for Erica. In this case, however, she uses the chronological format because virtually all of Erica's experience is in reference and applies directly to the position (see Figure 8-5). Note that Erica includes a position where she did intensive telephone work; while not library experience, it certainly demonstrates her flexibility and ability to deal with pressure.

Figure 8-1 Sample Recent Library School Graduate Resume: Newhouse

AUDREY NEWHOUSE
18 Copper Ridge Way
Potomac, MD 20859
301.243.1270
anewhouse@wellspring.net

OBJECTIVE	Librarian with an association or nonprofit organization.
QUALIFICATIONS	Expert searching skills using a wide range of databases. Reference experience with scientific and technical emphasis. Ability to work well in high pressure environment. Experienced Web searcher. Extensive writing and interviewing experience.

EXPERIENCE

Database and Technology Skills
- Extensive searching experience using Nexis Lexis, MedlinePlus, and OCLC Connexion system. Special emphasis on scientific and medical searching.
- Created and updated Web pages.
- Maintained publications database using Lotus Notes.

Reference and Bibliography
- As sole librarian for the Advisory Commission on Child Welfare and Nutrition, provided extensive reference service to nutritionists, doctors, and other researchers for scientific and technical information.
- Created bibliographies using a variety of online databases.
- Initiated interlibrary loans with other government agencies.
- Conducted in-depth telephone reference interviews with Maryland state legislative staff.

Library Support Services
- Weeded and conducted inventory of a technical library.
- Member of team that moved a library to another location.

Writing and Media Relations
- For member of Congress, wrote press releases and maintained media contacts.
- Responded to press inquiries and arranged interviews.
- Wrote articles for and designed newsletters.
- As newspaper reporter for *The Daily Progress* and *Town Crier*, wrote news and feature articles.

WORK HISTORY

2004–present	Librarian, Advisory Commission on Child Welfare and Nutrition
2004	Intern Technical Library, Wisconsin Comptroller of Public Accounts
2001–03	Information Specialist, Maryland State Legislative Reference Service, Telephone Inquiry Unit
2000–01	Press Assistant & Computer Operator/Press SecretarySenator Josephine S. Teller
1999–2000	Reporter, *The Daily Progress*, Asheville, NC
1998–1999	Reporter, *Town Crier*, Bishop, TN

(continued)

Figure 8-1   Sample Recent Library School Graduate Resume: Newhouse (*Continued*)

Audrey Newhouse, Page 2

EDUCATION

Master of Library Science, North Carolina Central University, Durham, NC, 2004.

Bachelor of Science in Mass Communications, East Tennessee State University, Johnson City, TN, 1994. Minor in political science. Cum laude.

VOLUNTEER WORK

2001, Montgomery County Public Library, Kensington Branch
- Shelved books, read shelves, and assisted patrons.

1991, National Endowment for the Arts, Washington, DC
- Conducted searches using library catalog.
- Provided information and referrals for grant applicants.
- Researched and responded to written requests for information.

PROFESSIONAL ORGANIZATIONS

Member, Special Libraries Association and American Library Association.

Figure 8-2   Sample Recent Library School Graduate Resume: Hazzard

Brandon G. Hazzard
1018 W. Tenth St.
Newark, NJ 07185
Office: 212-643-2305 Home: 212-443-5231
EMAIL: bghazzard@aol.com

Objective: Business Reference Librarian, Mansfield Library, University of Montana, Missoula, MT.

QUALIFICATIONS

- M.L.S. graduate with specialization in reference.
- Excellent background in business reference.
- Wide range of database skills.
- B.A. in business administration.
- Outstanding writing and presentation abilities.

EXPERIENCE

Reference

- Provided reference assistance in fast-paced Wall Street firm.
- Excellent knowledge of wide range of business reference sources.
- Completed significant coursework in business reference sources in library school.

Database Searching and Technology Skills

- Experienced searcher in many business and financial databases.
- Working knowledge of a wide range of software packages.
- Designed and maintained Web pages using HTML and XML.

Writing and Speaking

- Awarded prize for outstanding thesis.
- Experienced speaker at professional library association meetings.
- Assisted library school professor in the writing of *Business Reference Sources for Everyone.*

JOB HISTORY

Library Clerk (part-time), Harrison Forecasters, New York, NY, 2004–05.

Pizza deliverer, Tony's Pizzeria, Bronx, New York, 2004.

Sales Associate, Van Cleef & Arpels, New York, NY, 2003.

(continued)

Figure 8-2 Sample Recent Library School Graduate Resume: Hazzard (*Continued*)

Brandon G. Hazzard, Page 2

EDUCATION

Master of Library Studies, Queens College, Flushing, NY, 2005.

Bachelor of Arts in Business Administration, Long Island University, Brookville, NY, 2003.

DATABASE PROFICIENCY

Proficient in and routinely use a wide range of business databases including Bloomberg, Hoovers, Compustat, ABI/Inform, Factiva, ValueLine, Investext, and Business Source Premier.

PROFESSIONAL ACTIVITIES

New York Library Association
- Member, Business Round Table, 2004. Coordinated and led program on "Business Reference Sources on the Web."
- Treasurer, Legislative Day.

American Library Association
- Member: New Members Round Table and Library and Information Technology Association.

OTHER ACTIVITIES

- Reader, New York Tapes for the Blind. Read books and newspapers that are taped for the blind.
- Bird watcher, hiker, and skier.

Figure 8-3   Sample Recent Library School Graduate Resume: Bolanos

ALICIA C. BOLANOS
1365 W. Elm Ave. #B-5
College Park, MD 20793
Home: 301-254-4313   acbolanos@aol.com

Objective: Librarian I/Bibliographer for the Social Sciences and Journalism at the McKeldin Library, University of Maryland, College Park.

QUALIFICATIONS

- Master of Library and Information Science with coursework in collection development.
- Subject and expertise in journalism and social sciences.
- Experience working in an academic environment.
- Solid writing skills.
- Excellent search skills.

EXPERIENCE

Collection Development
- Undergraduate journalism degree with additional course work in economics, sociology, and government.
- Completed graduate course in collection development.
- Working knowledge of German.
- As reference intern in College Library, served students at reference desk.

Verbal and Written Communication
- As reference intern, extensive interaction with students in University Library.
- Wrote and administered an evaluation of University Library Skills Instruction Program.
- Regularly participated in German language discussion group.
- Spoke with wide range of clients as courseware developer.
- Wrote thesis entitled: *Collection Development in Women's History.*

Searching Skills
- Proficient searching skills including LexisNexis, Factiva, etc.
- Routinely performed electronic searches for college faculty.
- Excellent knowledge of electronic and Web sources in the social sciences.

WORK HISTORY

Reference Intern, College Library, University of Rhode Island, Kingston, RI, 2004.

Courseware Developer, Walcott-Taylor Company, Inc., Milwaukee, WI, 2003-04.

(continued)

Figure 8-3   Sample Recent Library School Graduate Resume: Bolanos (*Continued*)

Alicia Bolanos, Page 2

EDUCATION

M.L.I.S., University of Rhode Island, Kingston, RI, 2005.

B.A., Journalism, University of Wisconsin-Madison, WI, 2003. Graduated Cum laude.

PUBLICATIONS

- Assisted with research and bibliography for *Networking and Resources Sharing: Case Studies*, by Roger Bassett. Neal-Schuman Publishers, New York, 2001.

PROFESSIONAL ACTIVITIES

ALA Student Chapter
- Student Orientation Committee, 2004. Proposed to faculty that Student Association assist in the planning and implementation of fall orientation for new library school students. Served as chair of first committee.

Member: American Library Association, Special Libraries Association.

OTHER ACTIVITIES

- German Round Table—Regularly participate in activities related to German language studies.

- Enjoy Middle Eastern cooking, reading German literature, and listening to opera.

Figure 8-4   Sample Recent Library School Graduate Resume: Hemingway

Adam P. Hemingway

1220 Eastern Parkway, Brooklyn, NY 11203 • 718.822.5431 • aphemingway@aol.com

Objective: To work as Children's Librarian for Onondaga County Public Library, New York.

Qualifications

- M.L.S. with significant coursework in children's literature and library service to youth.
- Experience in working with children in public library.
- Volunteer reader for children's story hour.
- Excellent technology skills.

Experience

Service to Children
- Graduate coursework in children's literature and service to children.
- Current experience working with children in New York Public Library.
- Wrote thesis entitled *Kindergarten Library Program Enrichment*.
- Read in Saturday Story Hour for children.

Technology Skills
- Completed several graduate course related to technology.
- Searching experience using a wide range of databases.
- Completed independent study project on children's resources on the Web.

Job History

- Library Clerk (part-time), New York Public Library, New York, NY, 2004
- Administrative Assistant, Westover and Associates, New York, NY, 2002–03

Education

- Master of Library and Information Science, Pratt Institute, New York, NY, 2005.
- B.A., English, Oberlin College, Oberlin, OH, 2003.

Professional Involvement

New York Library Association
- Children and Young Adult Interest Group, 2004–05. Active participant on Annual Conference Program Subcommittee, assisting in the planning of 2004 program on "Diversity in Children's Literature."

New York Literacy Council
- Newsletter, 2005. Assist in the production and distribution of this publication.

Volunteer Story Reader, Brooklyn Public Library, 2004–05
- Regularly participate in Saturday Children's Story Hour.

Other Activities

- Swimmer, antiques collector, and cross-country skier.

Figure 8–5 Sample Recent Library School Graduate Resume: O'Neill

ERICA E. O'NEILL
825 Saul Road
Haverford, PA 19041-1392
Home: 610.333.4541 Cell: 610.232.5234
EMAIL: eeoneill@aol.com

Objective: To work as a reference librarian at La Salle University, Philadelphia, PA.

Qualifications

- Excellent reference skills.
- Experience working with undergraduate students.
- Broad range of database searching skills.
- Strong interpersonal skills.

Work Experience

Haverford College, Library

Temporary Reference Librarian, 2002–03
- Provided in-person reference service to undergraduate students.
- Extensive database experience including Lexis Nexis, Dialog, and the Web.
- Assisted in the development of user surveys to assess the quality of bibliographic instruction.
- Evaluated CD-ROM products on a regular basis.

Bibliographic Instruction Assistant, 2002
- Instructed groups of students on how to use a wide range of library sources (both print and electronic).
- Developed tip sheet on using Web sources.
- Compiled results of class evaluations.
- Provided in-person service to students using online sources.

The University of Pittsburgh, Hillman Library, Pittsburgh, PA

Reference Assistant, 2001–02
- Provided in-person and telephone reference assistance.
- Assisted professors with establishing reserve collections for class reference.
- Instructed students on use of Web sources.

Instruction Assistant, 2001
- Gave tours of library facilities.
- Assisted in student workshops on electronic sources.

(continued)

Figure 8-5 Sample Recent Library School Graduate Resume: O'Neill (*Continued*)

Erica O'Neill, p. 2

Regal Business Suites, Pittsburgh, PA

Administrative Assistant, 2000–01
- Answered telephone and took reservations for executive business suites company.
- Assisted up to 40 clients on an hourly basis.
- Received "Customer Service Excellence Award" for outstanding service.

Consulting Experience

- Prepared bibliography for inclusion in *The Single Mother* and *The Single Mother Sourcebook*, by Paula James (Apprentice Press, Pittsburgh, PA, 2002).
- Searched library and information science literature and prepared bibliography about evaluation of school library programs. For research conducted by Helen Eames, Associate Dean for Academic Studies, 2000.

Education

Master of Library and Information Science, University of Pittsburgh, Department of Library and Information Studies, Pittsburgh, PA, 2001.

Bachelor of Arts, German and History, Chatham College, Pittsburgh, PA, 1999.

Volunteer Experience

- Research Paper Clinic Volunteer, Undergraduate Library Services, Haverford College. Provided in-depth assistance to students during half-hour sessions on selection of appropriate sources and instruction in the use of those sources, 2002.

- Student Mentor Program, Pittsburgh, PA. Worked with high school students with learning disabilities, 2001.

Professional Activities

- Member, American Library Association.

9 SAMPLE RESUMES: SPECIAL LIBRARIAN

TIPS FOR THE SAVVY RESUME WRITER

- Avoid using library jargon and acronyms. Remember that the hiring official in a law firm or association may not recognize the significance of information that would be readily apparent to someone with a library background.
- Explain your position in straightforward language.
- Pay particular attention to quantifying your accomplishments when applying for corporate positions. Companies are bottom-line and results oriented.

MEET THE CANDIDATES

Tamara Conaway has had two jobs after library school and is applying for a position as assistant head in a large medical library. Note that she accounts for periods of unemployment (see Figure 9-1). The chronological format effectively showcases her relevant experience.

Maureen S. Cuevas is a law librarian with the federal government and seeks a senior position in a private law firm. She carefully considered both the functional and chronological formats, but decided on the chronological since she wanted to highlight her current job with the U.S. Court of Appeals (see Figure 9-2).

Deidre R. Bryan has lost her job due to a major downsizing in the nonprofit organization for which she works. She is applying for a position in an association library that does a significant amount of business reference. She has good skills that would be valuable in this setting. Because several of her most recent positions have been with education-related groups, Deidre thinks the functional format will highlight her accomplishments better than a chronological one (see Figure 9-3).

Nanci R. Wilkerson is a client representative with a well-known library vendor. She is now applying for a marketing and events coordinator position with a similar type of employer. Notice the emphasis on demonstrating her background in customer service, a key component of her desired position (see Figure 9-4).

The chronological format is effective in demonstrating her career progression.

Peter Fleming is seeking a position as director of a law library with a private firm. He chooses the chronological format since he can demonstrate good career progression that directly relates to this target position (see Figure 9-5).

Brooke Wyatt has gained excellent experience in the nonprofit area as a senior computer specialist. She wants to change focus and move into a corporate library environment (see Figure 9-6). Her technology and administrative skills are well-documented and clearly match the needs of the potential employer.

Tracy R. Napolitano has worked in one position as the sole librarian with a small association. She now seeks a better position as a trainer with a database company. Having chosen a functional format, note how well Tracy incorporates skills she has acquired in professional activities and outside interests (see Figure 9-7).

Margaret N. Talbott has acquired an impressive work history related to special collections cataloging. She chooses the chronological format to highlight the prestigious institutions where she has been employed (see Figure 9-8). Note how effectively she has documented professional memberships and activities, publications, presentations, and exhibitions.

Jeremy R. Hearne has a real challenge: He is seeking a supervisory position, but lacks extensive work-related experience in this area. To best highlight leadership experience he has acquired in professional and outside activities, he has chosen the functional format (see Figure 9-9).

Figure 9-1 Sample Special Librarian Resume: Conaway

TAMARA CONAWAY
Hermes International Information, Inc.
2142 Country Club Road
Chevy Chase, MD 20895
301-493-8888

OBJECTIVE: Assistant Head, Reference Section, National Library of Medicine, Bethesda, MD.

QUALIFICATIONS

- Highly skilled in all areas of science reference.
- Experience with a wide range of databases.
- Supervisory and administrative experience.
- Experience in managing large projects.

WORK EXPERIENCE

2000 to present: Information Specialist, Hermes International Information, Inc., Chevy Chase, MD

- Managed an extensive online patent information network consisting of over 6 million records.
- Authored three user database guides which have been integrated into overall commercial user manuals.
- Designed database fields and records.
- Supervised staff in testing pre-release versions of new systems.
- Directed all user liaison/customer support in the U.S.

1998–2000: Maternity leave

1996–98: Reference Librarian, Health Science Library, Georgetown University, Washington, DC

- Provided comprehensive reference services in a major medical library.
- Conducted high-priority medical reference research for acute-care and emergency services on "stat" basis.
- Developed comprehensive knowledge of biomedical reference services.
- Expert knowledge of science databases including Medline, General Science Index, Expanded Academic ASAP and ThomsonISI.

EDUCATION

M.L.I.S., San Jose State University, San Jose, CA, 1996.

B.A., Chemistry, Massachusetts Institute of Technology, Cambridge, MA, 1992.

(continued)

Figure 9-1 Sample Special Librarian Resume: Conaway (*Continued*)

Tamara Conoway, p. 2

PROFESSIONAL ACTIVITIES

- Member of peer review panel for the *Bulletin of the Medical Library Association*. Edited a special issue of the *Bulletin* on electronic publishing, 2003.

- Chair, Biological Sciences Group, Washington, D.C. Chapter, Special Libraries Association, 2000.

OTHER ACTIVITIES

- Treasurer, Parkwood Community Association, 2004–05.

- Competitive swimmer.

Figure 9-2 Sample Special Librarian Resume: Cuevas

MAUREEN S. CUEVAS
Library—U.S. Court of Appeals (5th Circuit)
601 Camp St.
New Orleans, LA 70130
Cell: 504.717.2423

OBJECTIVE: A senior position in a private firm law library.

SUMMARY OF QUALIFICATIONS

- Supervisory experience in a law library.
- Broad knowledge of all aspects of law library operation including reference, databases, technical services, and cataloging.
- Significant budgetary and planning experience.
- Experience in providing high quality service to clients.

WORK EXPERIENCE

Senior Librarian/Trainer, Library of the U.S. Court of Appeals (5th Circuit), New Orleans, LA, 2001–present

- Coordinated program for information resources in 20 Circuit libraries.
- Trained library staff in cataloging and classification.
- Administered ILS implementation, database training, FEDLINK, and private contracts.
- Oversaw budget for cataloging and Attorney Admission Fund.

Senior Law Librarian/Head of Technical Services, Law Library, San Francisco State University, San Francisco, CA, 2000–01

- Established and monitored the acquisition and cataloging procedures (RLIN).
- Supervised and trained six staff members.
- Administered budget for the technical services department.
- Taught Lexis Nexis classes to staff and students.
- Served as Acting Director of the Law Library.

Senior Cataloger, Shared Cataloging Division, Library of Congress, Washington, D.C., 1995–2000

- Performed descriptive cataloging of materials in English, French, German and Hungarian.
- Trained new catalogers in an apprenticeship program which lasted three months.
- Served as a member of the Name Authority Cooperative (NACO), the national program for authority work.

(continued)

Figure 9-2 Sample Special Librarian Resume: Cuevas (*Continued*)

Maureen S. Cuevas, Page 2

EDUCATION

- Master of Science, Southern Connecticut State University, Department of Information and Library Science, New Haven, CT, 1994.
- Bachelor of Arts, French, Princeton University, Princeton, NJ, 1992.

DATABASE AND TECHNOLOGY SKILLS

- Proficient in Blackboard 5, Dreamweaver, Excel, Lexis Nexis, Lotus, OCLC, PowerPoint, RLIN, Westlaw, basic Microsoft applications, HTML.

HONORS

- Recognition Award, U.S. Court of Appeals (5th Circuit), 2003, 2005.

- Outstanding Performance Award, Library of Congress, 1998, 1999.

PUBLICATIONS

- Collaborator, *International Law Pathfinder* [electronic resource]. New Orleans: Office of the Circuit Librarian, 2005 (in progress).

- Editor, *The Fifth Circuit ILS Cataloging Manual.* New Orleans: Office of the Circuit Librarian, 2004.

- "Catalogul in secolul 21: viitorul bate la usa" [The Catalog in the 21st Century: The Future is at the Door] in *Proceedings of the National Seminar on Libraries, Archives, and Information Centers in the 21st Century* (1997: Brasov and Targu-Mures, Romania). San Francisco, 1997.

PROFESSIONAL ACTIVITIES

- Faculty Member, National Conference of State Legislatures, Annual Meeting, 2005.

- Delegate, White House Conference on Library and Information Science, Washington, D.C., 2004.

- Library Fellow, United States Information Agency/American Library Association, Spring 1997, Central University Library, Budapest, Hungary.

- Guest/participant, East-West Summit on Emerging Computer Technologies in Libraries, International Centre for Scientific Information, Helsinki, Finland, 2002.

- Member: American Association of Law Libraries, American Library Association, Northern California Association of Law Libraries.

Figure 9-3 Sample Special Librarian Resume: Bryan

DEIDRE R. BRYAN

1905 Queen Street * Alexandria, VA 22302 * 703.966.2225

OBJECTIVE   Position as an Information Specialist with the American Bankers Association.

QUALIFICATIONS
- Able to work well in high pressure environment.
- Experienced manager of association information centers.
- Excellent skills in acquisitions, cataloging, and serials control.
- Expert searcher in a wide range of databases.

EXPERIENCE   **Reference Support**

- Four years experience as sole information center librarian, provided wide range of reference service to public service agencies.
- Developed bibliographies on numerous topics.
- Coordinated clipping services for current awareness packets.

Technology and Database Searching

- Implemented and maintained acquisitions, cataloging, classification, and loan procedures using INMAGIC software.
- Developed databases for training records and mailing lists.
- Experienced searcher with LexisNexis, Dialog, ProQuest, Westlaw, the Web, BNA Publications, InfoTrac, and Factiva.

Collection Development

- Selected, acquired, and processed a multi-media collection for a resource center.
- Managed a large clearinghouse of information related to education policy.
- Reviewed and annotated new titles under consideration for purchase.

WORK HISTORY			
	2002–04	Director	Resource Center, Human Rights Welfare League, Bethesda, MD
	2000–02	Manager	Information Services, Education Now Foundation, Alexandria, VA
	1997–2000	Librarian	Takoma Park Branch, Montgomery County Public Library, Takoma, MD
	1994–97	Librarian	U.S. Committee for Petroleum Awareness, Washington, DC

(continued)

Figure 9-3   Sample Special Librarian Resume: Bryan (*Continued*)

Deidre R. Bryan, Page 2

EDUCATION	M.A., Library and Information Science, University of South Florida, Tampa, FL, 1993.
	Bachelor of Arts in Sociology, Sweet Briar College, Sweet Briar, VA, 1990. Graduated Magna cum laude.
AWARDS & HONORS	• Beta Phi Mu Honor Society, 1993.
	• *Who's Who Among Students in American Universities and Colleges*, 1989–90.
PROFESSIONAL ACTIVITIES	• Member, American Library Association and Special Libraries Association.
	• District of Columbia Library Association
	Membership Committee, Chair, 2004–05.
	Member of Board of Directors, 2003–04.
	Chaired the Joint Spring Workshop, 2003. Coordinated one-day program, "Legislative Advocacy," which was attended by over 100 librarians.

Figure 9-4   Sample Special Librarian Resume: Wilkerson

Nanci R. Wilkerson

694 Sunset Blvd.
Los Angeles, CA 90215
Office: 323.441.2424 * nrwilk@dotzero.org

OBJECTIVE: To work as a Marketing and Events Coordinator with Bristol Library Corporation.

HIGHLIGHTS OF QUALIFICATIONS

- Broad experience in customer service.
- Knowledge of marketing in the field of librarianship.
- Experience in planning and implementing client programs in library environments.
- Master's degree in library science.

WORK EXPERIENCE

Client Representative, Vista Library Services, Los Angeles, CA, 2001–present

- Managed three large accounts including California Alliance of Research Libraries.
- Reviewed all major documentation produced by training team.
- Directed all aspects of Vista's Annual Users Group Meeting.
- Represented VISTA at national conferences.

Coordinator of Library Technology, Hearst Foundation Library, Los Angeles, CA, 2000–01

- Managed all aspects of technology networks, PC's, telecommunications, multimedia systems, and system security software.
- Planned and implemented new circulation system.
- Supervised two full-time employees and hourly assistants.

User Services Librarian, Fielding Enterprises, Inc., Costa Mesa, CA, 1998–2000

- Served as acquisition specialist, with additional concentration in cataloging/authority control, serials, and overlay processing.
- Performed training sessions on a regular basis.
- Assisted clients in troubleshooting any problems.
- Improved service by designing online client profile to track problems.

Reference Librarian, Loyala University Library, Chicago, IL, 1998

- Provided in-person and telephone reference service with emphasis on business.
- Taught patrons to use a variety of electronic sources.
- Reviewed training manuals for reference support staff.

(continued)

Figure 9-4 Sample Special Librarian Resume: Wilkerson (*Continued*)

Wilkerson, Page 2

Project Manager, Africana Retrospective Conversion Project, University of Illinois, Chicago, IL, 1997

- Oversaw retrospective conversion of Africana materials from the Jason R. Tannon Collection (approximately 20,000 volumes).
- Prepared all authority work.
- Supervised 2.5 staff and hourly assistants.

EDUCATION

M.S., Library Science, University of Illinois, Urbana-Champaign, 1997.

B.A., Economics, Stanford University, Palo Alto, CA, 1993. Graduated cum laude.

PROFESSIONAL AND OUTSIDE ACTIVITIES

Special Libraries Association
- Chair, Advertising and Marketing Division, 2003-04. Coordinated publication of directory of libraries providing advertising reference.
- Member, Information Futurists Caucus.

Oregon Outdoors and Fishing Association
- President, 2004-05.

Figure 9-5 Sample Special Librarian Resume: Fleming

PETER S. FLEMING

42 W. Crystal Drive
Arlington, VA 22202
Cell: 703.788.4282 * Home: 703.245.1422

Objective: Director of a library for a private law firm.

Qualifications

- Extensive experience in managing all areas of a law library.
- Experience in supervising staff.
- Outstanding background in all areas of law reference.
- Known for emphasis on superior client service.

Work Experience

Head of Legislative Services; Pasekoff, Farber, & Pettavino, Washington, D.C., 2003–present

- Provided reference service to 180 attorneys.
- Trained and supervised three legislative assistants.
- In-depth knowledge of LexisNexis, Westlaw, LegalTrac, Legal Periodicals and Books Index, Factiva, and Dialog.
- Devised and implemented Web training program for the entire firm, including weekly work shops and daily one-on-one training for attorneys.
- Collected and distributed all relevant legislative material.

Branch Supervisor, City of Charlotte Law Library, Charlotte, NC, 2000–03

- Managed 18,000-volume collection.
- Provided reference service to attorney and judicial clients.
- Performed all collection development duties for the branch.
- Established policies and procedures for staff and patrons.
- Planned a move from a 3,000-square-foot space to a 6,500-square-foot space.
- Cited as "City Employee of the Year" for 2001 for excellence in service to the city.

Law Librarian; Mauzy, Hevener, & Scott, Charlotte, NC, 1998–2000

- Sole librarian for 50 attorney branch office of a large Atlanta law firm.
- Performed all legal and nonlegal reference and research using a wide range of electronic resources.
- Performed all administrative functions including collection development, budgeting, coordinating MCLE training for attorneys.
- Supervised looseleaf filing service.
- Planned and developed a new library space and implemented the move.

(continued)

Figure 9–5   Sample Special Librarian Resume: Fleming (*Continued*)

Peter S. Fleming, Page 2

Education

M.L.I.S., University of South, Columbia, SC, 1997.

M.A. in Journalism, Columbia University, New York, NY, 1995.

B.A. in Journalism, Hunter College, New York, NY, 1991.

Professional Activities

American Association of Law Librarians
- Speaker, Annual meeting in Pittsburgh, Program on "Training Reference Librarians," 2003.

Law Librarians Society of Washington, D.C.
- Secretary/Treasurer, 2000–01.

Figure 9-6   Sample Special Librarian Resume: Wyatt

BROOKE G. WYATT

1300 Innsbruck Way, Potomac, MD 20854
Office: 202.433.2940   Email: brooke@aol.com

JOB OBJECTIVE: To manage a large corporate library with a strong technology focus.

QUALIFICATIONS

- Expert Web manager and designer.
- Strong leadership skills and experience in leading teams.
- Excellent interpersonal skills.
- Commitment to providing quality service to clients.

WORK EXPERIENCE

Senior Computer Specialist
American Heritage Institute, Washington, DC, 2002–present.

- Webmaster for two major Web sites: the AHI site with 2000 reports and an internal staff site.
- Led a team of four professional staff.
- Maintained and reported all statistical analysis of Web site usage.
- Coordinated all user support.
- Designed and implemented enhancements to the Web site.

Special Projects Librarian
Georgetown University Library, Washington, DC, 1999–2002.

- Led team that planned a fee-for-service document delivery program.
- Headed a pilot project on a new graphical interface for the in-house OPAC.
- Tested the feasibility of OCLC's EPIC service as a reference tool.
- Assisted in hiring, training, and supervising of the program coordinator for the computer-based reference services program.

National Science Foundation Grant, Online Research Project
School of Information and Library Science, University of North Carolina at Chapel Hill, 2001.

- Team member of project which studied online search strategies of librarians in North Carolina and Virginia to replicate steps for an electronic process.
- Assisted in soliciting librarians to participate in the project.
- Analyzed data according to a theoretical artificial intelligence.
- Received certificate of appreciation for outstanding work.

EDUCATION

Master of Science in Library Science, University of North Carolina at Chapel Hill, 2001.

B.A., English, Elon University, Elon, NC, 1999.

(continued)

Figure 9-6   Sample Special Librarian Resume: Wyatt (*Continued*)

Wyatt, p. 2

PUBLICATIONS

- "Career Alternatives: How to Expand Your Library Career," *District of Columbia Library Association Newsletter*, June 2005.

- "Oh What a Tangled Web We Weave," Library Journal, October 2005, pp. 41–45.

PRESENTATIONS

- Special Library Association, annual conference, Los Angeles, 2002. Environment and Resource Management Division, "Supporting Networks Through Indexing and Metadata: The New Data Frontier." Participated with two other panelists from Oxford University and the National Biological Information Infrastructure project.

- District of Columbia Library Association, Workshop, 2004. "The Internet: the Good, the Bad, and the Controversial."

PROFESSIONAL INVOLVEMENT

District of Columbia Library Association

- Technology Special Interest Group chair, 2005. Planning a spring 2006 program on conducting a Web site usability study.

- Legislative Committee, member, 2004.

American Society of Information Science

- President, Washington chapter, 2002.

OTHER SKILLS AND ACTIVITIES

- Fluent in German and Spanish.

- Rowed and sailed up the Inside Passage from Anacortes, WA to Juneau, AK, 2000.

Figure 9-7   Sample Special Librarian Resume: Napolitano

TRACY R. NAPOLITANO

88 N. Crescent Way
Tysons Corner, VA 22095
Office: 703.223.1515   Email: trnapo@aol.com

OBJECTIVE

To work as trainer for LexisNexis.

QUALIFICATIONS

- Skilled in training and developing training programs.
- Knowledge of a wide range of databases.
- Excellent writing and communication skills.
- Able to manage multiple demands in deadline-oriented environment.
- Master of Science in Library and Information Science.

ACCOMPLISHMENTS

Training

- Developed a training program for users of SearchMagic databases in a networked environment.
- Trained volunteers to be adult literacy tutors.
- Taught basic reading skills to adults.

Technology

- Developed library databases including a book catalog.
- Redesigned InMagic reports and databases to better meet user needs.
- Designed and implemented an Internet Gopher.
- Maintained electronic book and serials catalog.

Communication Skills

- Wrote abstracts for biweekly association publication.
- Developed materials to promote member services.
- Led committee on intellectual freedom for local library association.
- Edited the newsletter of the Washington Literacy Council.

WORK HISTORY

Senior Information Specialist, National Video Association, 2004–present

Senior Sales Associate, Pottery Barn, 2003–04

(continued)

Figure 9-7   Sample Special Librarian Resume: Napolitano (*Continued*)

Tracy R. Napolitano, Page 2

EDUCATION
Master of Science in Library Science, University of Tennessee, Knoxville, TN, 2002.

Bachelor of Arts, Computer Science, Johns Hopkins University, Baltimore, MD, 2000.

PROFESSIONAL ACTIVITIES

- Chair, Intellectual Freedom Committee, District of Columbia Library Association. Coordinated major program for Banned Book Weeks.

- Fairfax County Literacy Center: Certified Tutor, 2004; Certified Trainer, 2005.

- Member, Special Libraries Association.

Figure 9-8 Sample Special Librarian Resume: Talbott

MARGARET N. TALBOTT

The Ocampo Center for the Study of Art
2412 Gatehouse Road
Greenwich, CT 06831
203.243.1542 * mntalbott@earthlink.net

OBJECTIVE: Director of a university archives or special collections.

QUALIFICATIONS

- Extensive experience in archival processing and cataloging.
- Broad knowledge of technology applications for special collections cataloging.
- Supervised a large staff of catalogers.
- Nationally recognized for work related to special collections management.

PROFESSIONAL EXPERIENCE

Head of Collections Cataloging, The Ocampo Center for the Study of Art, Greenwich, CT, 2003–present

- Managed archival cataloging and processing of manuscripts, photographs, and archives.
- Supervised 17 subject specialists.
- Extensive technology and database knowledge.
- Served on Project Coordination team to select an integrated library system.

Special Collections Librarian, Manton Department of Special Collections, Main Library, San Jose State University, San Jose, CA, 2000–03

- Provided reference service for collection including a photo study collection of over 2 million items.
- Supervised Title II-C and California State Library Cataloging Grants.
- Specialized in Hispanic collections, including the North Collection on the Spanish Civil War and the Baja California Collection.
- Served as technology liaison with library.
- Coordinated online catalog implementation for special collections.

Consultant (6-month project) to The Ocampo Center for the Study of Art, Greenwich, CT, 1999–2000

- Developed a processing, cataloging, and preservation plan for the Raymond Loewy collection consisting of 2 million drawings, diagrams, posters, and books.
- Developed and implemented database identifying all Loewy design projects.

(continued)

Figure 9-8   Sample Special Librarian Resume: Talbott (*Continued*)

Margaret N. Talbott, Page 2

Cataloger, Photographs Division, Corcoran Gallery of Art, Washington, DC., 1998–99

- Cataloged master photographs for internationally known collection.
- Supervised archival processing and microfilming projects.
- Assisted in revision of the Corcoran Gallery of Art Thesaurus for Graphic Materials.

Bibliographer II, Hispanic American Periodicals Index, San Jose State University, San Jose, CA, 1997

- Indexed Spanish, Portuguese, French and English language journal articles relating to Latin American history, politics, and culture.
- Revised thesaurus and completed substantial name authority work.

EDUCATION

Master of Library and Information Science, University of California, Los Angeles, 1995.
- Specialization in cataloging and classification, including advanced courses in cataloging theory and practice, subject analysis, non-print cataloging, and acquisitions.

Graduate coursework in Latin American Studies, San Jose State University, 1993–94.

Intensive Portuguese Institute, University of California, Los Angeles, Summer, 1992.

A.B. in Spanish, San Jose State University, San Jose, CA, 1993.
- Included studies in Spain (Univ. Complutense, Madrid).

LANGUAGES

Fluent in Spanish and Portuguese. Reading and writing knowledge of French and Italian.

PROFESSIONAL MEMBERSHIPS AND ACTIVITIES

Society of American Archivists
- Member, Nominating Committee, 2004.
- Mentor Program Volunteer, 2002.
- Publications Board, 2001.
- Member, Committee on Archival Information Exchange, 1999–2000.

(continued)

Figure 9-8   Sample Special Librarian Resume: Talbott (*Continued*)

Margaret N. Talbott, Page 3

American Library Association
   Association of College and Research Libraries, Rare Books and Manuscripts Section
   • Chair, 2004–05.
   • Executive Committee, 2002–03.
   • Preconference Program Planning Committee, 2000–02.

   Librarians' Association of the University of California
   • Professional Development Committee, 2004–05.
   • Statewide Research Committee, 2002–03.

Member: Art Librarians's Society of North America, Visual Resources Association, and Online Audiovisual Catalogers.

PUBLICATIONS

"Description for Digitized Photo Archives." Published in *Image Access Project: Proceedings from an RLG Forum*, held in Monterey, CA. Mountain View, CA: Research Libraries Group, 2003.

"Cataloging Archival Photograph Collections," *Visual Resources*, v. 11 (2002), pp. 85–100.

"Rare Book Catalogers and Technology," *Rare Books and Manuscripts Librarianship*, v. 7, no. 2 (2002), pp. 70–75.

"Problems in Subject Classification in Special Format Materials." Co-authored with Steve Noll. Published in *Subject Indexing in Context* by Pat Turner, Boston: Prentice-Hall, 2000.

CONFERENCE PRESENTATIONS

"The Digital Image Access Project," invited paper, Society of American Archivists, Phoenix, AZ, September, 2004.

"Processing Archival Photograph Collections," invited speaker, Seminar on Images in Libraries and Museums, Portland, OR, 2002.

"Descriptive Cataloging of Rare Books," Seminar chair and speaker, Rare Books and Manuscript Section Preconference, Orlando, FL, 2001.

"Guidelines for Library Special Collections," invited speaker, University of California Conference on Photographic Collection Administration, Pasadena, CA, 2000.

(continued)

Figure 9-8   Sample Special Librarian Resume: Talbott (*Continued*)

Margaret N. Talbott, Page 4

OTHER PROFESSIONAL ACTIVITIES

Panelist, National Endowment for the Humanities, November, 2004.

Instructor, Visual Materials Cataloging course. Columbia University, Rare Book School, 2002.

Archives Consultant, American School of Victorian Studies, London, 2001.

Invited participant, Council on Library Resources, symposium on form and genre terminology for thesauri, New Haven, CT, 2001.

EXHIBITIONS

"Images of Spain from the Manton Department of Special Collections," Main Library, San Jose State University, 2004.

"Dreams and Design: Drawings from the Raymond Loewy Collection," The Astor Center for the Study of Art, 2000. Selected, mounted, and documented exhibit.

Figure 9-9   Sample Special Librarian Resume: Hearn

Jeremy R. Hearne

Library of the Maryland General Assembly
90 State Circle
Annapolis, MD 21401
301.804.3344 * jrhearne@vista.net

Objective: Position as Supervisory Librarian in the Maryland General Assembly.

Qualifications

- Demonstrated leadership skills in a wide range of positions.
- Extensive reference and technology background.
- Outstanding interpersonal skills.
- Committed to providing the best client service possible.

Skills and Accomplishments

Leadership and Supervision

- Served as Acting Supervisor of Library of the Maryland General Assembly for four months—supervised 8 employees.
- Led committee to choose vendor for network.
- Coordinated all conference programs for the Maryland Library Association.
- Chaired team that visited each member of the General Assembly to solicit information needs.
- Served as President of college alumni association.

Reference

- Provided telephone and in-person reference to members and staff of General Assembly.
- Experienced searcher in wide range of database including LexisNexis, Factiva, Westlaw, Datatimes, and Web.
- Assisted with collection development of the "hotline collection."
- Specialized in searching sources related to business in Maryland.

Work Summary

Information Research Specialist, Library of the Maryland General Assembly, Annapolis, MD, 1995–present

Research Analyst, Virginia Department of Commerce, Richmond, VA, 1993–95

Library Technician, University of Richmond Library, Richmond, VA, 1992

(continued)

Figure 9-9   Sample Special Librarian Resume: Hearn (*Continued*)

Jeremy R. Hearne, Page 2

Education

M.L.S., Syracuse University, Syracuse, NY, 1991.
B.A., Business Administration, University of Rhode Island, Kingston, RI, 1990.

Professional Activities

Special Libraries Association
- Chair, Government Relations Committee, 2000-01.

Maryland Library Association
- Member, Library Legislative Day Committee, 1998-99.

President, Syracuse University, School of Information Studies, Syracuse, NY, 2003-04.

Part III

Interviewing Successfully

10 WRITE THE COVER LETTER THAT GETS THE INTERVIEW

In this chapter we are going to examine how to successfully tailor a cover letter, a task that some resume writers find especially difficult to complete. To simplify the process, we'll break it down in several steps and use Janet Taylor as an example. But first, let's consider the various ways the employer evaluates the cover letter.

EMPLOYER'S COVER LETTER CRITERION

CHECK YOUR WRITING ABILITY

The cover letter demonstrates your grasp of the written word, and for positions in which writing ability is a critical element of the job, the cover letter is sure to be scrutinized carefully. Like the resume, the employer will view this as your first work product.

CHECK YOUR READING ABILITY

A cover letter indicates to the employer whether you have read the job posting or announcement correctly. Are you able to match your skills and qualifications with the stated needs of the employer?

SCREEN FOR THE BEST CANDIDATES

As Steve Theodore ("Read the Darn Ad," *Game Developer*, May 2005, p. 44) so aptly states, "The cover letter makes sense when seen against the backdrop of the two basic rules of hiring. The screener or HR person who reads your application is trapped between two desires: to find a great candidate, and to dispose of all the no-hope candidates as efficiently as possible. The cover letter helps the screener in both directions."

JOB CANDIDATE'S COVER LETTER GUIDELINES

> Keep the cover letter short and to the point. One page is usually best since employers don't have time to read more.

Does every employer read the cover letter? Probably not, but you still want the best letter possible just in case. As we examine each step, keep these guidelines in mind: Keep the cover letter short and to the point. One page is usually best, since employers don't have time to read more.

- Use it as an opportunity to demonstrate your knowledge of the library or organization to which you are applying; show that you have done your homework.
- We've said it once, but it bears repeating. The employer will use this letter to evaluate your writing skills.
- Show the employer how your experience relates to the job, focusing on how your skills will benefit the employer. What is the added value you bring to the position?
- Specifically address the required qualifications if you are responding to an advertisement.
- The tone of the letter should be conversational. Avoid stilted language and make it upbeat, positive, and enthusiastic.
- Quantify when possible. Numbers paint pictures and employers like to know results, so mention the number of employees you supervised, how much money you saved the library, etc.
- The cover letter provides you with an opportunity to reveal your personality.
- Just like the resume, check and recheck for typos, grammar, and neatness.
- Ask others—colleagues, mentors, managers—to review the cover letter just as you would the resume.

ADDRESS AND SALUTATION

Place your address and the date at the top right margin. Below that, at the left margin, give the name and address of the person or organization you're contacting. Exercise caution when you don't know the name of the hiring official; this often happens when you are applying for a position listed in a newspaper or professional journal that asks you to respond to "Search Committee" or "Human Resources Department." Never assume the gender of the individual you are addressing. When you are unable to ascertain an appropriate name, a phrase such as "To whom it may concern" or "Dear Search Committee" or "Dear Employer" is the best alternative.

Janet Taylor wants to apply for the following job:

Library Director. Public Library of Youngstown and Mahoning County serves a population of 260,000, with a staff of 75, main library, 4 branches, and a budget of $8.5 million, in a university community. We seek a dynamic leader who puts service first and has proven communication skills, financial expertise, and knowledge of library technology. Must be effective with library board, public officials, library support organizations, and the community. Qualifications: MLS from an ALA accredited program and 5 yrs. professional management experience in a public library. Submit letter and resume to: Audrey Johnson, Youngstown Public Library, 305 Wick Avenue, Youngstown, OH 44503.

In applying for this specific job opening Janet Taylor uses the following salutation:

27 Chelsea Court
Woodland Springs, AR 72764
May 1, 2005

Audrey Johnson
Youngstown Public Library
305 Wick Avenue
Youngstown, OH 44503

Dear Ms. Johnson:

THE OPENING PARAGRAPH

In the first paragraph, say why you are writing (state the name of the position) and how you learned of the opening. If you have been referred to the individual by a mutual acquaintance, be sure to indicate the name. But do so, only if you have obtained per-

In the first paragraph, say why you are writing (state the name of the position) and how you learned of the opening. If you have been referred to the individual by a mutual acquaintance, be sure to indicate the name. But do so, only if you have obtained permission to do so.

mission to do so. You can also use a "hook" sentence to immediately grab the reader's attention. This sentence should describe how your qualifications relate to the specific position. It can also identify a unique ability, skill, or knowledge that would be especially desirable to the employer. The first paragraph can also provide an opportunity to demonstrate your knowledge of the target library or organization, as we shall see in one of the sample resumes.

Here is Janet Taylor's opening paragraph:

> I am writing in response to your advertisement for the position of Library Director for the Public Library of Youngstown and Mahoning County, which appeared in *American Libraries*, April 2005. As an Assistant Director in a rapidly growing public library system like Youngstown, I offer strong leadership and management experience as well as a solid record of community involvement.

The second sentence provides that attention-grabbing hook— Janet successfully draws a parallel between her library experience and that of the target position.

THE SECOND PARAGRAPH

Before writing this paragraph, carefully review the qualifications in your resume and focus on the two that are most important –in other words, those that best sell you to the employer. Think carefully about how your skills and abilities meet the needs of the library, paying particular attention to the job posting or announcement. Again, demonstrate what you know about the library or organization. You might also indicate why you are attracted to the position or library or organization—for example, your record of strong community outreach, the innovative use of technology, or the rapidly expanding public library system.

Here is Janet's second paragraph:

> You will note in my resume that I have experience in virtually every area of public library administration. As part of a team that manages over 100 employees and a budget of $4 million, I bring strong skills in strategic and fiscal management.

Remember, keep thinking like the employer—what will be of greatest interest to their library?

THE CLOSING PARAGRAPH

End your letter with thanks and indicate what you would like to happen next. For example, request an interview, say that you will be calling, or that you would like to meet at the employer's earliest convenience.

Here is Janet Taylor's closing paragraph.

> End your letter with thanks and indicate what you would like to happen next. For example, request an interview, say that you will be calling, or that you would like to meet at the employer's earliest convenience.

> Thank you for your consideration of my resume. I would like to tell you more about my accomplishments and how I can help serve the Youngstown and Mahoning County library patrons. Please contact me on my cell phone at 501.555.1415, or I will phone you later next week.
>
> Sincerely,
>
> Janet F. Taylor

Your cover letter should have the same typeface as your resume and should be printed on the same type of high-quality paper. Now, let's take a look at some other cover letters for resumes in this book.

SAMPLE SUCCESSFUL COVER LETTERS

Remember, the cover letter should be short, no more than one page, and showcase your strongest qualifications.

LANAHAN COVER LETTER FOR LIFE SCIENCES LIBRARIAN POSITION

Kenneth Lanahan is applying for a position as life sciences librarian in the science library, Antioch College. In addition to an M.L.S. degree, the position requires "academic degree or extensive experience in science; demonstrated knowledge of Web and electronic information resources; and excellent oral and communication skills." Look at Figure 10-1 to see how skillfully Kenneth has used these buzzwords to describe why he is best suited for the position.

Figure 10-1   Lanahan Cover Letter

84 Oak Court #C-1
Knoxville, TN 03210
February 29, 2006

Antioch College
Science Library
Yellow Springs, Ohio 45387

Dear Search Committee:

I have enclosed my resume in response to your recent advertisement in *The Chronicle of Higher Education* for the position of Librarian-Life Sciences in the Antioch Science Library. With more than four years experience as an academic science librarian, I am especially well-suited to working in Antioch's library environment, one that *Technology Today* recently described as among the most innovative in the United States.

In addition to completing an M.L.S., I have a graduate degree in zoology. My career has focused on providing a high level of service to clients: first to 50 corporate scientists and presently to students in a busy science library. In all of these positions, I have used a wide range of science databases and provided expert technology support.

I would welcome the opportunity to discuss my qualifications for this position and I appreciate your consideration of my resume. Please phone me at 704.555.9415, or I will contact you next week.

Sincerely,

Kenneth Lanahan

ANDRUS'S COVER LETTER FOR LIBRARIAN I/BIBLIOGRAPHER POSITION

Madeline Andrus has just graduated from library school and is applying for her first professional librarian position. She is applying for Librarian I/Bibliographer in social sciences and journalism in an academic library. The position requires working with instructional and research faculty in the college of journalism, developing effective collection strategies, knowledge of European language, and the ability to communicate effectively. Although Madeline doesn't have a great deal of professional experience, she has demonstrated her major skill areas quite well in the cover letter in Figure 10-2.

Wow! You've come a long way! Now your well-written cover letter and excellent resume have landed you a job interview! Move on to the last chapter for ways to present your best face and put your best foot forward.

Figure 10-2   Andrus Cover Letter

311 W. Chestnut Street
Milwaukee, WI 53222
May 3, 2006

Helen Walden
Undergraduate Library
University of California, Los Angeles
Box 2445
Los Angeles, CA 94115

Dear Ms. Walden:

I am responding to your advertisement in *Library Jobline* concerning the position of Librarian I/Bibliographer in Social Sciences and Journalism in the Undergraduate Library. My strong communication skills and subject expertise in journalism are particularly well suited to this position.

With a B.A. in journalism and an M.L.I.S. with coursework in collection development, I have provided extensive reference service to university students and enjoy the challenge of a busy reference desk. My writing and bibliographic skills have been honed as technical writer.

I am anxious to learn more about this position and how my broad range of skills can be of service to the Undergraduate Library. Thank you for reviewing my resume. I can be reached during the day at 414-225-4313, or will contact you in the near future.

Sincerely,

Madeline C. Andrus

11 ESSENTIALS OF INTERVIEWING

PREPARE TO INTERVIEW

With that job-winning resume, you've made it to the interview stage. Congratulations! Now that you've got your foot in the door, the interview is the opportunity to really sell yourself. Even if you don't have an interview scheduled yet, this is a good time to start thinking about this stressful process. Under the best of circumstances, interviewing is not an easy task. A survey by OfficeTeam of 1,000 executives nationwide revealed some of the strange but true things that occurred in interviews: (Cullen, Scott, "Inhumane Resources," *Office Systems* 13:10 (Oct. 1996), p.6):

- One candidate arrived at the interview in a suit—with price tags dangling from the sleeve.
- An interview was scheduled to be held in Decatur, Illinois—the job applicant showed up in Decatur, Georgia.
- During the interview the applicant's cellular phone rang—and she answered it.

Sound amazing? Trust me, most seasoned interviewers could quickly add similar items to the list. And never underestimate the creativity of employers to come up with some, ahem, new and off-the-wall interview questions. Reporter Amy Joyce recounts that a director of sales asked interviewees about their favorite Pepperidge Farm cookie. Her rationale for posing this question: "My department is very fast-paced and unpredictable, and I ask that question to find out how well they think on their feet . . . if there's just a blank stare, then stammering—or worse, they think I'm joking—then that tells me quick thinking might not be a strong suit, and I'll pursue that with other questioning." (*Washington Post*, Oct. 17, 2004, "Deciphering the Handwriting on the Wall," F5). While we may not be able to prepare you for every possible question an employer may pose, we will do our best to help you feel prepared and less stressed when you get to the interview table.

Think of the interview process as being a two-way experience. The employer will use the interview to learn as much about you as possible—your experience, training, education, accomplishments, and professional activities. Beyond evaluating whether or not you have the right skills and abilities to actually do the job, the employer wants to assess if you will be a good fit in the library. In other words, will you play well in the sandbox? Do you have the type of personality that the employer perceives will work well in the organization?

Don't forget this is *your* opportunity to learn about the library and make sure this is where you want to work. What is the staff like? What is the character of the working environment? To whom will you be reporting? Is he or she someone with whom you can work productively? Will this position further your career goals?

I am frequently surprised that job applicants will devote many hours to resume writing but completely neglect interview preparation. Now is not the time to rest on your laurels and leave the interview process to chance! Feeling well prepared will greatly increase your confidence level when you arrive for the interview. Getting ready for the interview will be hard work, but the time you invest in this process will be well worth it. And we are going to use the same approach we used for writing your resume by guiding you step by step through everything you need to do to prepare for your interview. Think of yourself as being in training for the Interview Olympics, and remember that only one contestant will get that gold medal: the job!

> Feeling well prepared will greatly increase your confidence level when you arrive for the interview. Getting ready for the interview will be hard work, but the time you invest in this process will be well worth it.

In this section we will cover the following:

- Preparing for the interview—conducting research about your potential employer, anticipating questions and practicing responses, and recommendations for what to wear.
- At the interview—interview style and protocol, techniques for answering questions, managing salary issues, and posing questions to the interviewer.
- After the interview—thank-you letters, references, and second interviews.
- Special types of interviews—informational, screening, telephone, group vs. one-on-one, and meal-time interviews.
- Interview tips—essentially, Interview 911—if you only have limited time to prepare, these tips and reminders can be interview lifesavers.

CONDUCT TARGET EMPLOYER RESEARCH

> It is important to know as much as possible about the library or organization before the interview, as well as those who will be conducting the interview.

It is important to know as much as possible about the library or organization before the interview, as well as those who will be conducting the interview. Occasionally, the employer will provide you with background information at the time the interview is scheduled. The more data you are armed with, the better prepared you will be. After all, you are a librarian, so doing research should be a breeze! Your research provides you with better insight into the interview questions. It also helps inform the questions that you may want to pose to the interviewers. You will likely find opportunities to reference this research during the interview. For example, you might preface a question with, "According to your most recent annual report" or "In reading an

article about your library in *Library Journal*, I learned that . . ."
This quickly demonstrates to the employer that you have done
your homework and are genuinely interested in learning more
about the organization.

There are many places to consult to learn more about your
potential employer. Traditional sources include newspapers and
magazines, the library Web site, as well as other sites on the Web
which may contain public information. But to really learn as much
as possible, I recommend using your personal network. Individuals who currently or formerly worked for the library can be
goldmines. Don't forget to use your professional network and
contact colleagues in local and national professional organizations. If they don't have the information you need, they often have
friends or colleagues who do. You may be surprised to find that
the library community is a very small world. I'm frequently contacted by job seekers inquiring about individuals I know through
my professional association involvement who might provide more
information about their target library. Colleagues are often very
forthcoming with this information.

It is also important to go armed with as much background as
possible about salary. Professional association Web sites, such as
the American Library Association and the Special Library Association, provide a wide range of excellent resources about salaries in different types of library positions.

ANTICIPATE INTERVIEW QUESTIONS AND ANSWERS

Anticipating the types of questions that will be posed to you is
one the most important parts of preparing for the interview. This
section lists some of the most common and predictable questions
that interviewers may pose. Interviewers generally focus on two
categories of questions:

- Behavioral, which focus on your personal behaviors and
  qualities.
- Situational, which focus on choices you make about specific problems and how you go about solving them.

In preparing for the interview, you should review these questions and add your own based on your knowledge and research

about your target position and library. In some cases we have provided some sample responses that may help guide your thinking about these responses. With other questions, you will want to bullet your own experiences and examples. Don't memorize these responses; rather, have a general sense of how you will respond and have specific examples in mind based on your own experience. Again, providing specific examples is key, since employers are focused on results.

The questions below are divided into six groups with some overlap:

- Employment history,
- Personal characteristics,
- Skill-related,
- Hypothetical,
- Managerial,
- Entry level or new librarian.

EMPLOYMENT HISTORY

These tend to focus on your background and provide the employer with an opportunity to clarify information in your resume.

What do you like most/least about your present job?

This is a question that can quickly lead you down the garden path. In terms of what you like about your current job, focus on those activities that best mirror those in the target position. As to weaknesses, don't, under any condition, ever criticize your current employer or coworkers even when it is justified. References to difficult supervisors, indifferent upper management, lazy coworkers, etc. will not be well received. In terms of what you like least about your present job, try a response like this:

> *The thing that I most dislike about my present job is the lack of opportunity to learn new skills or to take on new challenges. I enjoy my work and feel I make a positive contribution to the library, but I've been able to master the major duties and now seek greater responsibility and opportunity.*

Why have you been in your current job so long?

If you have been in the same job for a long time (over five years at the nonmanagerial level), employers will zero in on this factoid immediately. Your challenge is to take this negative question and turn it into a positive. In some cases, there are many good reasons for staying in a position for an extended period. For example,

> *Although I have been in the same position for six years, I have been fortunate to have excellent opportunities for growth. My duties have expanded in many areas and I received several outstanding performance ratings. While I still enjoy the position, I am ready to further expand my skills and serve in a new role with greater responsibility.*
>
> *During the past several years, there have been significant reductions-in-force in my library due to budget cuts. Hiring has also been frozen. I enjoy my work and been loyal to the institution, but I now seek a new opportunity with more stability and new opportunities.*

If you have been in the same job for a long time (over five years at the nonmanagerial level), employers will zero in on this factoid immediately. Your challenge is to take this negative question and turn it into a positive.

Can you explain these long gaps in employment?

There are many plausible reasons for employment gaps. These include attending school, child care, caring for elderly parents, illness, etc. But if the gap was because you had problems finding a job, be honest about it and describe your efforts to find a position. You might also state that the time unemployed allowed you to reassess your goals. As a result of that assessment, you are now more focused in your job search and ready to take on a new position.

Don't you think you are overqualified?

You're thinking, "Yes, but I really like to eat and pay the rent." The employer is obviously concerned that you might only stay in the position for a brief amount of time. So the trick is to focus on the opportunity which the targeted position creates. You might respond:

> *There are other positions at a higher level that I could pursue, but I'm impressed with the opportunities created by this position and I feel I can make a significant contribution here. This is the type of institution where I feel I can learn and grow.*

Where do you see yourself in five years? What are your long-term career objectives?

What the interviewer really means is, "Just how long do you plan to stay in this position should we hire you?" Employers generally want a multiyear commitment given the amount of time and resources it takes to recruit and hire people today. Also, budgets have become vulnerable and employers feel this might be a "last chance" to hire before a freeze, so inquiries about employee longevity are inevitable. It does not pay to be coy in responding to this question. A good answer might be:

> *I see myself in a dynamic library or organization where I can grow and learn professionally, take on new challenges, and make the type of contribution I think I'm capable of delivering. From what I have learned so far, this is just the type of library where I could achieve those goals and make a long-term commitment.*

Why have you changed jobs so often?

Or if the interviewer was being really truthful, he or she might query, "Why can't you keep a job?" This question is most often raised with those who are fairly junior in their careers. There are a number of plausible reasons why someone has job-hopped. A typical answer might be:

> *After graduating from library school, I did move around in some entry-level positions. While I was not in any one position for an extended period, I did gain a broad range of skills. I am now more focused on where I want to go professionally and am seeking a long-term commitment.*

Have you ever been asked to resign? Why were you fired?

If you have been asked to resign or been terminated from a position, you know this question is coming, so there is no need to squirm in your seat. This is the one answer you should memorize. Be honest and direct with your response, but don't belabor the question or go into too much detail. Again, don't criticize your former employer under any circumstances. If there were problems, acknowledge them in a forthright manner. Then emphasize how you have learned from them and how you have since improved your performance. In other words, focus on the future. There is no reason to linger over this answer. Put it out there and then move on.

PERSONAL CHARACTERISTICS

Tell me about yourself.

This interview question has been around since the earth cooled, so expect it to pop up in one form or another at the beginning of the interview. Intended as an icebreaker or warmup, don't be misled by the informal nature of the question. Take this question

> First impressions are always important, so think of your response in these terms. Remember that people listen fairly intently for the first five minutes of any presentation and then rapidly tune out.

very seriously. First impressions are always important, so think of your response in these terms. Remember that people listen fairly intently for the first five minutes of any presentation and then rapidly tune out. The general nature of the question provides an excellent opportunity to showcase the skills you want to sell to the interviewer or those abilities that might set you apart from other candidates. A good response might be:

Since graduating from library school with a concentration in Web development and instructional design, I have held several positions that have used these skills to help deliver high quality service to a variety of public library patrons. I'm someone who is very goal oriented, works well under pressure, and thrives under tight deadlines. In my spare time I enjoy coaching field hockey for my daughter's team and playing tennis.

Adding something personal, such as nonwork pursuits, can help provide the interviewer with the "big picture" you. Remember that your response to this question should be brief. Don't feel that you have to describe every qualification or skill set. Many interviewees deplete all of their good examples with this question and have nothing new to offer later in the interview.

How would you describe your strengths and weaknesses?

This question that should have been mothballed years ago, but is a perennial favorite of many interviewers. Occasionally, it actually reveals some interesting data from unsuspecting job candidates who are far too forthcoming about their weaknesses. Remember that this is not the moment for true confession. There really is such a thing as too much information. Citing strengths should be fairly straightforward: Put yourself in the employer's shoes and think about strengths that make you best qualified for the position. Identify the strength and then follow up with a specific example. For example:

> Citing strengths should be fairly straightforward: Put yourself in the employer's shoes and think about strengths that make you best qualified for the position. Identify the strength and then follow up with a specific example.

One of my strengths is the ability to manage multiple projects at the same time. For example, in the past six months I was responsible for planning and implementing a move of the library's special collections to an off-site location in preparation for a major renovation. The original deadline became much more compressed and I had two less weeks to complete the move. I was also responsible for hiring two new reference staff which had to be hired before the end of the budget year. Through good planning and my ability to manage the moving team, I was able to meet both deadlines.

Weaknesses, however, require more careful consideration. Avoid responding "none." Everyone has some weaknesses, and this response will make you look a bit swell-headed at the very minimum. Rather, focus on some situation where you were able to learn and improve on your performance. Here are some sample responses:

From time to time, I become frustrated with myself when I don't meet my professional goals in the amount of time I think I should attain them. I set high standards for myself and those around me. So I've learned to set realistic goals and monitor my progress, but not become frustrated if I don't meet every goal when I think I should.

In the past, I sometimes tended to take on too many projects at work. In one case I came close to not meeting an important deadline. That experience taught me the importance of planning and allowing for the unexpected.

How do you handle stress?

The correct answer is not "When in trouble or in doubt, run in circles, scream and shout." Take this opportunity to demonstrate that you work well under stress. You might also give examples where you actually *thrived* under stress. For example,

Stress is inevitable in any fast-paced work situation. My positions have frequently involved tight deadlines with attendant high stress. I don't let stress prevent me from doing a good job. I break projects down into manageable components, assess the resources needed to complete the project, and develop an action plan to complete the project within the deadline required.

What is the best way to motivate you?

This is not the moment to focus on salary, benefits, or the size of your new office. Rather, highlight those things that showcase you as a go-getter. For example:

I'm motivated by new challenges and the opportunity to apply what I do best, but also to learn new skills. I'm also motivated by working with other people who share the same goals, vision, and passion for delivering outstanding service.

Why is this position appealing? Why do you want to work here?

Here is your golden opportunity to effectively link your knowledge, skills, and abilities with what the employer needs. A response might be:

I am anxious to put my experience of managing people together with my extensive knowledge of cataloging. I'm especially attracted to working in a dynamic library like this one.

SKILL-RELATED

Skill-related questions focus on just that, your experience and qualifications in the major skill areas required by the job. Your focus should be on providing specific examples that most clearly demonstrate the breadth and depth of your qualifications.

Discuss a situation or project where you have worked under a tight deadline.

Be sure to include specific examples and describe the steps you took to meet those deadlines.

Discuss a situation where you have worked on or led a team.

Be sure to be specific about your role on the team. Describe your contribution and don't forget to discuss the outcome of the work of the team. How did your team make a difference to the library? What product did it deliver? How did it improve service?

What do you do to stay current in your area of librarianship? Are you active in any professional organizations?

I'm frequently amazed at how casually job candidates treat this question. This is your golden opportunity to demonstrate your commitment to the profession. Employers want staff who keep up with new developments in the field and are well networked in the library community. Be sure to mention any professional reading, attendance at conferences, and any other association or professional activities.

Figure 11-1 provides examples of good answers to some difficult questions.

Employers want staff who keep up with new developments in the field and are well networked in the library community. Be sure to mention any professional reading, attendance at conferences, and any other association or professional activities.

Figure 11-1   Weak vs. Strong Answers to Difficult Questions

If asked how did you manage a difficult situation you've encountered, focus on a specific example and demonstrate how it has helped you grow professionally.

TELL US ABOUT A TIME WHEN YOU . . .
  worked effectively under pressure

Weak answer: I'm really good at working under pressure most of the time.

Strong answer: Stress has been a component of virtually all my positions and I thrive under pressure. For example, in my current job I had only two months to implement a major upgrade in the online catalog. I developed a plan, determined which resources were required, and got to work. Working with my staff, we managed to implement the upgrade a week ahead of schedule.

  anticipated potential problems and developed preventative measures

Weak answer: It's always hard to know what problems might come up, but when they do I generally know how to deal with them. I'm a great problem solver.

Strong answer: As part of my project planning, I always try to lay out what problems might evolve over the course of the project. I like to involve other staff in this process in order to anticipate the potential pitfalls. When these potential issues are defined and analyzed, I then factor these into the entire planning process.

  had to deal with an irate customer or patron

Weak answer: You can always count on some patron to stir up trouble. I'm usually pretty successful at calming them down.

Strong answer: I have had significant experience with customer service in my job as a first-line reference librarian in a public library. First, I try to listen carefully to the patron's problem and express empathy. Then, I focus on finding a solution. Also, I follow up with the patron on any unresolved issues.

  had to adapt to a difficult situation

Weak answer: I'm really very talented at dealing with difficult situations. They come up all the time in my present position, and I always deal with them with great dispatch.

Strong answer: Yes, difficult situations come up in many positions, so I try to find the best strategy to deal with them. For example, our staffing budget was recently cut by 10 percent. Needless to say, staff were very concerned about layoffs. My first effort was to meet with staff to try to allay their fears, quell rumors, and discuss how we would deal with this crisis. Next, I met with our budget officer to examine options. We were able to implement some cutbacks in other areas that

(*continued*)

Figure 11-1   Weak vs. Strong Answers to Difficult Questions (*Continued*)

---

prevented us from laying off many staff. Unfortunately, some staff were laid off, but I think our strategy minimized the number of staff affected.

surmounted a major obstacle

Weak answer: I have had to surmount a number of major obstacles in my recent position. For example, I have a number of coworkers who are not team players, so it has been frustrating to get my work done. I just try to avoid them.

Strong answer: I was assigned to lead a team that seemed to be going in many different directions and had low morale. It was having a big impact on productivity. I realized quickly that individual team members were not aware of their colleagues' activities. So I set up regular meetings with agendas. This definitely helped with project coordination. Improving morale was a bigger task and took more time to accomplish. But I developed some strategies that helped. For example, when the team met certain goals, I brought in pizza to celebrate. I also promoted having an article about our team included in the staff newsletter. This provided greater visibility about the project in our library and greatly enhanced the status of the team.

made the wrong decision

Weak answer: That's a tough one, I'm not sure I recall a recent example where I really made a wrong decision.

Strong answer: In my last position as a children's librarian, I made a wrong decision in scheduling story hours. I didn't consider the best times when parents could bring their children and attendance was very low. In the next schedule cycle, however, I did research on past programs and implemented a short survey. This experience really taught me about planning and doing thorough research before making a decision.

managed multiple projects or tasks

Weak answer: I can juggle a million things. Just ask anyone I work with—I can manage lots of big projects and always complete them on time.

Strong answer: I feel I'm especially adept at juggling multiple projects. Here is a recent example. I manage a small law library. I was involved in providing data for a really important case that had a tight deadline. In the midst of this, another large case requiring library support came up with another hard deadline. To meet both deadlines, I quickly reassigned staff from other projects. I negotiated with another manager in the firm to borrow a staff member for a week. We worked long hours, but successfully met both deadlines.

Hypothetical questions are the "what if" and "how would you handle this situation" types of questions. They are generally designed to test your problem-solving skills and to test your ability to react to a specific situation. They are especially popular with managerial positions.

HYPOTHETICAL

Hypothetical questions are the "what if" and "how would you handle this situation" types of questions. They are generally designed to test your problem-solving skills and to test your ability to react to a specific situation. They are especially popular with managerial positions. These questions are typically posed like this:

- How would you react if a patron asked for a particular book to be removed from the collection?
- If your acquisition budget was cut by 10 percent, how would you make decisions about what would be eliminated?
- If a contractor was not completing work in a timely manner, how would you handle it?
- How would you manage a situation where a patron was looking at inappropriate material on the Internet?
- If you could select only ten reference sources in your area of expertise, what would they be?

These questions are obviously hard to anticipate, and are definitely worthwhile thinking about carefully. The most important thing to communicate is the *process* you use for decision-making —For example, how you gather information, consult with others for input, monitor and adjust the outcome of the decision, etc.

MANAGERIAL POSITIONS

The following questions present a range of topics that are often the focus of managerial interviews. In thinking about good responses, remember to use specific examples that will paint a picture for the employer.

Summarize your professional managerial experience.

How many employees do you supervise? How many direct reports do you have?

How do you motivate staff?

How do you communicate with staff?

What experience do you have in strategic planning?

Have you ever fired an employee?

Have you dealt with staff dealing with personal problems?

What is the largest budget you have managed?

How many employees have you supervised? How many direct reports?

Describe your management style.

Do you have public speaking experience?

What are the three most important issues facing (type of library) today?

Tell us about a time you hired the wrong person for the job.

What techniques would you use to evaluate service quality and customer satisfaction with services provided?

How would you deal with an irate customer that complains to you about poor services that he/she just received?

What experience have you had in introducing new technologies?

How do you keep up with new developments in the library world?

Do you have experience working with a unionized workforce?

What experience do you have in preparing and administering a budget?

What methods or techniques do you use to determine staffing needs in the library?

What is the most difficult personnel situation you have dealt with? How did you manage it? How was it resolved?

How do you manage employee performance evaluations?

ENTRY-LEVEL OR NEW LIBRARIAN

Thinking about potential questions for entry-level or new librarians is especially important since most will have limited direct experience. Remember to consider all of your experience, not just that acquired in a professional position. Draw on volunteer or professional association activities or skill sets acquired in non-professional positions. For example, positions where you may have

> Thinking about potential questions for entry-level or new librarians is especially important since most will have limited direct experience. Remember to consider all of your experience, not just that acquired in a professional position.

worked under pressure or with a wide range of people—skills that greatly benefit a professional position.

Tell us about your last job or practicum. What types of responsibilities and duties where you given on that job?

If you are a new graduate, which courses in your master's program related directly to this position? What courses did you like best and why?

What do you think the (school, public, academic, etc,) library of the future looks like?

Do you have any favorite Internet sites?

Do you currently subscribe to electronic mailing lists? If so, which ones?

Have you discovered any ideas that were particularly helpful?

What would you do if you heard a colleague give out incorrect information or misstate a library policy?

What are your thoughts about Internet filtering?

When you were in library school, did you plan on working in a (type of library)?

If you have previous library experience, what is the most important thing you have learned from that experience?

INTERVIEW DRESS REHEARSAL

> Spending some time rehearsing for your interview in advance will definitely lower your blood pressure when you get to the interview table. Practicing ahead of time will help you relax and feel more comfortable.

Spending some time rehearsing for your interview in advance will definitely lower your blood pressure when you get to the interview table. Practicing ahead of time will help you relax and feel more comfortable. Think of yourself preparing to go onstage. Using your list of prepared questions and bulleted answers, find a partner to pose questions to you and practice saying the answers. At first you will feel very awkward, but better here than at the actual interview. It is also helpful if your "stand-in" interviewer is someone who can also critique your responses. If you can't find a partner, rehearse your responses alone.

As you are practicing, don't try to memorize answers; this will only cause more stress when you get to the real interview. Another dress rehearsal tip is to dress in the clothes you plan to wear at the interview. Some job applicants anxious to make a good impression wear new or seldom worn outfits to the interview. To prevent any wardrobe malfunctions, try road-testing your wardrobe in advance.

One of the best resources for interview role playing is *The Interview Rehearsal Book: 7 Steps to Job-Winning Interviews Using Acting Skills You Never Knew You Had* by Deb Gottesman and Buzz Mauro (New York: Berkley Books, 1999). These actor/authors provide you with many tips that will help you with breathing, voice, and confidence. As the author's point out, "Nothing is more important in an interview than the actor's specialty: self-presentation. Your skills and qualifications may have gotten you in the door, but it's your personality—the winning way you *present* your skills and qualifications—that will get you the job. You only get one chance to make a great impression, so you've got to let the interviewer see you at your best."

QUESTIONS TO ASK THE INTERVIEWERS

Nine out of ten interviewers pose this question to the applicant at the end of the interview: "Do you have any questions about the position?" I am always amazed when an applicant states: "No, I think you have covered everything." This is a great opportunity for you to learn more about the library and to demonstrate your curiosity and enthusiasm about the position. And retrieving a page of questions from your portfolio will make a great impression and illustrate that you took the time to plan ahead. This is not the time to ask about salary or benefits, the size of your office, or your reserved parking space. Rather focus on substantive questions about the library and the position.

Again, remember that an interview is a two-way street and this is your opportunity to interview the interviewers to see if the position is the right fit for you. Knowing when to stop asking questions is more art than science. Clearly, you will want to watch the clock as well as the interviewer's facial expressions and body language to be sure that you don't overextend this opportunity.

Following is a list of questions to consider. They are divided into three general categories: questions about the position, the library, and the hiring process.

Questions About the Library
What are major challenges facing this library?

> Again, remember that an interview is a two-way street and this is your opportunity to interview the interviewers to see if the position is the right fit for you.

What do you like best about your job with the library?

What is the work culture like? Collegial? Collaborative?

Questions About the Position

Is this a new position?

Regarding the person that was last in this job, what is he or she doing now?

What is the most important thing you would like me to accomplish in the first six months on the job?

Are there opportunities for training and professional development?

What is a typical day like?

Hiring Process Questions

What are the next steps in the hiring process and what is your time frame?

Will there be second interviews?

What is your timetable for selection for this position?

Who can I ask about the status of this position?

DRESS THE PART

Much ink has been spilled on the interview wardrobe. Simply put, let common sense prevail and always err on the conservative side. Your favorite tie with the smiley faces or that black leather jacket may be the "real" you, but the interview setting is not a fashion runway. You don't have to be a Stepford wife, but finding an outfit that works well with the library culture will definitely serve you best. Here is a checklist of wardrobe tips:

For men:

- A dark, conservative suit is a always a safe bet.
- A suit generally makes a more positive statement than a sportcoat.
- A plain shirt with a contrasting tie generally works well.
- Keep the tie conservative.

For women:

- A dark, conservative suit or pantsuit is always a safe bet.
- Avoid bold patterns in clothing.
- Use makeup conservatively.
- Use jewelry sparingly—no dangly earrings, clanking bracelets, or rings on every finger.

For both men and women

- Resist wearing perfume or after-shave; people can be sensitive or allergic to certain scents.
- Good grooming is a must including neat hair and nails; avoid any attention-getting nail polish.
- Make sure your clothes are freshly pressed.
- Avoid bold patterns and colors.
- Shoes should be shined and conservative.
- Teeth should be freshly brushed.
- No smoker's breath.
- Avoid any problematic foods, such as onions or garlic, before the interview.

As discussed previously, make sure you rehearse your outfit. You should be totally comfortable with how your outfit "acts."

INTERVIEW LOGISTICS

There are a number of other things you will need to do in preparation for the interview. First and foremost, check out the location of the interview. If you are not familiar with the location, go in advance so you know the room location exactly. Nothing will fluster you more than trying to locate it at the last minute.

Here's a tip about some very basic information you want to have about the interview panelists before you arrive for the interview. When you are contacted for the interview, ask the spelling and punctuation of every panelist name. Also, their titles if possible. This will save you having to learn this at the interview table. Remember, everyone likes to have their name pronounced correctly. The accurate pronunciation of an especially difficult name will definitely win you points.

Always plan to arrive for the interview at least ten minutes early. Remember, arriving late is the kiss of death! I've heard every excuse—traffic was heavy, the subway broke down, I was in an accident, I was chased by a pack of hungry wolves—and none is acceptable for arriving late. An employer will assume that if you can't make it on time for an interview, you won't show up for

Always plan to arrive for the interview at least ten minutes early. Remember, arriving late is the kiss of death!

work on time. Make sure you allow for any traffic delays or time to find a parking space. Be sure to bring extra copies of your resume with you, since the panelists may have forgotten or lost your resume, and make sure you have enough for each interviewer. Also, bringing copies of writing samples and work products always makes a good impression. Again, make sure you have one for each interviewer.

One hopes that the employer will provide you with a glass of water, but just in case, be sure to stick a bottle of water in your briefcase for an attack of dry throat. Here's a surefire tip to keep your voice from getting hoarse during the interview: Squeeze some fresh lemon juice in your water bottle. It really works!

DELIVER A JOB-WINNING INTERVIEW PERFORMANCE

The interview day has arrived and you are feeling well-prepared having completed all of the steps in the last chapter. This section will cover:

- protocol for starting the interview,
- your personal interview style,
- tips for answering interview questions,
- questions about salary, and
- concluding the interview.

PROTOCOL FOR STARTING THE INTERVIEW

Remember that from the moment you walk into the library, you are being evaluated. The receptionist or secretary greeting you at the front door may later share his or her impressions of you with those individuals doing the hiring. So it pays to smile and be confident from the moment you enter the room. When you are contacted to schedule your interview appointment, make a point of being especially polite and accommodating. If you are ushered into a personal office for the interview and you have a few private moments, take note of any objects or things on the wall that might help you make a personal connection with the interviewer. Be sure to ask if all the interviewers have a copy of your resume.

If you are seated and the interviewers come into the room, make sure you stand with good posture to greet them. First impressions count, and you want to be your best right from the beginning. Smile, appear confident and dynamic, look them straight in the eye and give them a firm handshake. A note on handshakes: They should be firm, not bonecrushing. And by all means, avoid the limp or "dead fish" handshake. Nothing is a bigger turnoff than a weak handshake.

As I mentioned before, it is always best to ascertain the names of those who will be interviewing you before the actual interview begins, and you should also confirm the correct pronunciation of their names. If this is not possible, you may want to repeat the names of your interviewers when you are introduced. Again, if you are unsure about pronunciation, don't hesitate to ask. Once you are seated, you may want to jot down the names on paper.

Before the interview begins, there may be an opportunity for some small talk. Remember, there is no such thing as "small" talk. The evaluation clock has started ticking, so you should make the most of this. Use it as an opportunity to learn something about your interviewer. Be upbeat and make sure you maintain good eye contact. This seemingly casual interaction is a way for your interviewers to observe you in a social situation; they will be thinking how you might similarly interact with employees, patrons, and donors. That said, keep in mind that most interviewers are not out to get you or lead you into a trap. Most are truly on your side and understand that they have a role in selling the job to you.

Once you are seated, be sure to put a pen and a pad of paper on the table and have your portfolio with your prepared follow-up questions handy. However, take notes sparingly and make sure this doesn't become a distracting activity during the interview.

DEVELOPING YOUR PERSONAL INTERVIEW STYLE

Remember that interviewers are looking for someone who will be the right fit with their library or organization, so your style and personality are very important. They want someone dynamic and enthusiastic, who displays a positive attitude. Here are some tips to help you convey that positive image:

- Do your best to smile and look pleasant. This may feel like the Spanish Inquisition, but try to make it look like a walk in the park. And as a former interview coach once advised me, "Don't sweat!"
- Your facial expressions and body language signal a great deal about how you feel. Do your best to look relaxed, but alert and comfortable with the situation.
- Speak slowly and clearly. Don't race through answers gasping for breath.

> Don't be afraid to pause. It shows that you are thoughtful and reflective. When you are asked a question, don't feel that you have to launch in with an answer immediately. Using a pause is also a good way to collect your thoughts if the question is especially difficult.

- Don't be afraid to pause. It shows that you are thoughtful and reflective. When you are asked a question, don't feel that you have to launch in with an answer immediately. Using a pause is also a good way to collect your thoughts if the question is especially difficult.
- Feel free to ask the interviewer to repeat the question. If the question throws you for a loop, stall for time by using this tactic.
- Avoid "ums" and "you know" as much as possible.
- Make sure you engage *all* of the interviewers. This can be challenging, depending on how they are seated, but do your best to make eye contact and keep them all fully engaged with what you are saying.
- Don't fidget or play with your jewelry, hair, or clothes.
- Here is the most important tip you may learn from this book: know when to stop talking. I can't reiterate this enough. Many job applicants don't know when to stop. Nothing—repeat, nothing—will make interviewers tune out faster than a job applicant who drones on and on. This is especially important with the first question of the interview; some interviewees feel they must recount every experience and example in the first question. Don't fret. You'll have plenty of opportunity later in the interview.
- Pay attention to the body language and nonverbal cues of your potential employers. When they start to yawn, nod off, fidget, or look at their watches, you know you need to wrap it up.

ANSWERING INTERVIEW QUESTIONS

While we have examined the types of questions you might encounter in interviews, here are some general tips and guidelines for responding to questions:

- Use specific examples whenever possible to illustrate your knowledge, skills, and abilities.
- When asked about your work on teams or how you contributed to a project, be specific about your role. If you led a team, say so. If you served on a team, be specific about your contribution.
- Whenever possible, quantify your answers. It demonstrates that you are results and bottom line oriented. It also quickly conveys the scope of what you are describing. For example, indicate the number of employees you supervised, how many questions you answered at the reference desk, how performance improved as a result of your efforts, etc.

> Whenever possible, quantify your answers. It demonstrates that you are results and bottom line oriented. It also quickly conveys the scope of what you are describing.

- With trick questions, such as being asked to describe weaknesses, use a good example and then show how you learned from it and improved your performance.
- Never say anything critical or negative about yourself.
- As we discussed in the last chapter, be direct and succinct when handling questions about terminations or other sensitive topics. Be honest and then focus on what you learned from the experience. In some cases, it may be appropriate for you to raise the sensitive issue if you feel that it will inevitably be asked. This approach can demonstrate positive qualities about candor and directness.
- Never, ever criticize your current employer or reveal any proprietary or confidential information.
- This is not the time to be modest so don't underestimate your yourself. At the same time, always be honest.
- When appropriate, refer to sources you have consulted about the target library. For example, "In a recent news article about the library, it was noted . . ."
- Mention current trends in the field that may pertain to the library. This shows you are curious and professionally aware.

STUMPED FOR AN ANSWER?

This is probably your worst interview nightmare. The interviewer poses a question and he or she might as well be speaking a foreign language. Several things may cause this: You are nervous and simply go blank; the question is so out of left field that it totally confuses you; or, you truly don't know the answer. How should you manage this Twilight Zone scene?

- Pause. Just pause and collect your thoughts. You don't have to rush into the answer. There is nothing wrong with a few moments of silence. Rather, sit back, look thoughtful, and collect your thoughts.
- Stall. If you don't understand the question or it catches you off guard, ask follow-up questions for clarification. This is a great delaying tactic. It won't make you look stupid and may actually highlight your analytical and inquiring qualities.
- Apologize and acknowledge you don't know the answer. This is the absolute worst-case scenario, but it beats making up the answer, which will certainly commit you to the first ring of Dante's hell. If you recover later and can answer the question, raise it at the end of the interview with a lead-in like this: "If possible, I would like to return briefly to a question you asked me earlier."

You have several options for responding to illegal or inappropriate questions. For example, queries about marital status, sexual orientation, religious preference, children, health, etc. First, this may tell you a good deal about the character of your potential employer and make you run for the hills. Again, the interview is an opportunity for you to learn about the employer. You can also challenge the interviewer, but be aware that this will likely squelch your chances for the position.

HANDLING QUESTIONS ABOUT SALARY

With questions related to salaries, it is always preferable to wait until the job offer is on the table and avoid asking about salary at the first interview. But it is certainly advisable to determine what you are worth before the interview. There are a number of good sources to consult:

- Job advertisements in publications like *American Libraries* and the *Journal of Higher Education*
- Salary surveys on the American Library Association and Special Libraries Association Web sites

Clearly, you are in the best position to negotiate when the job is offered. In the event the question is posed at the first interview, try to defer it by indicating that you want to learn more about the job and the library. If it appears that you will annoy the employer by evading the question, then by all means do respond. You can then ask for the salary range for this type of position and ask for details about the complete compensation package. Another appropriate question is to ask about opportunities for advancement.

CONCLUDING THE INTERVIEW

At the end of the formal interview, you have several opportunities to really sell yourself. The interviewer will no doubt ask if you have any questions. You want to be sure to pull out a list of questions from your portfolio to indicate that you have thought about the questions in advance. Some of the questions discussed in the earlier chapter may be appropriate. This is also the opportunity to return to an earlier question which you may have not fully answered. For example, you might want to say, "I would like to return just a moment to a question you asked earlier about leadership."

Following the questions, the interviewer will likely ask if there is anything else you want to say to show that you are a strong candidate for the position. This is the moment to end with a re-

> With questions related to salaries, it is always preferable to wait until the job offer is on the table and avoid asking about salary at the first interview. But it is certainly advisable to determine what are you worth before the interview.

Following the questions, the interviewer will likely ask if there is anything else you want to say to show that you are a strong candidate for the position. This is the moment to end with a really strong finish.

ally strong finish. First, thank the employer for the opportunity to interview for the position. Be sure to state clearly, if this is truly the case, that you want the job. Then, sum up your strengths based on what you have learned during the interview. Try to link your qualifications and accomplishments to the goals stated by the employer during the interview. This is the moment to leave them begging for more.

You may be offered the opportunity to tour the library. Express curiosity and greet everyone you meet cordially.

FOLLOWING THE INTERVIEW

Now that the interview is over, you have additional opportunities to make a good impression. Immediately follow up with a thank-you note to each interviewer, not just the selecting official. This should be typewritten, and it is best to use good stationery—i.e., paper that has a significant cotton content. If you can hand-deliver the letters the next day, all the better. Some candidates use e-mail, but generally speaking, the hard copy letter makes a much better presentation. After thanking the interviewer, use the letter to highlight your skills and abilities that best meet the job expectations as they have been described to you. The letter should be succinct and to the point. A typical letter might read:

Dear Mr. Ford:

Thank you for the opportunity to interview for the position of Information Services Librarian with San Diego State University. After learning more about the position, I am convinced that I have the skills to contribute to the dynamic environment I observed in your library.

With nearly five years of experience in providing reference service with print and electronic information sources in a similar academic environment, I feel I have the ability to meet your priorities. The prospect of working with the library's electronic classroom technology is especially exciting. I have extensive experience in designing and implementing online instructional courses. My work on these courses at Ball State University was recognized with a meritorious service award.

Again, I appreciate the opportunity to meet with you. If I can provide further information, please don't hesitate to contact me.

Depending on how the employment process progresses, at some point you will be asked for references. You obviously want to

> Depending on how the employment process progresses, at some point you will be asked for references. You obviously want to choose references who are accessible and articulate about your background and qualifications. Never, ever, give out the name of a reference without asking for permission first.

choose references who are accessible and articulate about your background and qualifications. Never, ever, give out the name of a reference without asking for permission first. Make sure you give correct contact information; nothing is more frustrating than trying to track down a reference whose telephone number has changed or is no longer at that place of employment. It is especially helpful to references if you alert them that they might be called about a certain position for which you have interviewed. You should inform them about the job and the types of things that might be useful to raise in a conversation about you. Having well-prepared references might just give you the edge you need to get the job.

If you are called back for a second interview you should follow the same routine as preparing for the first interview. Second interviews are generally less structured and provide you with another opportunity to ask questions. A tour of the library and further staff introductions may be part of this as well.

SPECIAL TYPES OF INTERVIEWS

In this chapter we will examine some special types of interviews. These include informational, screening, panel vs. one-on-one, meal-time, and telephone interviews.

INFORMATIONAL

Informational interviews are one of the best, but frequently overlooked, methods of finding a job. Typically, an informational interview is just that—an opportunity to seek information, advice, and referrals from an employer separate from a formal employment process. The interview can result from a contact you have made through networking or can be a cold contact. Take advantage of the fact that employers in the library world are generally very willing to talk to potential job candidates and provide advice about a job search. Remember that people love to give advice and often feel quite flattered to be asked.

Whether or not you have narrowed your search to the type of library you want to work in or have a specific organization in mind, take advantage of your network to find a contact for an informational interview. Individuals in your local library association or other professional association are great sources of information. If this approach doesn't produce a useful contact, you can always try making a cold contact within the library.

The ideal way to begin this process is to have someone in your network approach the individual in the library where you want an informational interview. Your network individual can make the first introduction and arrange for you to call the contact. If this is not possible or you must make a cold contact, a letter requesting the interview is the next best thing. Choose decision-makers and those with hiring authority. You might try a letter like the following:

Dear Ms. Williams:

I am a recent library school graduate and am exploring various areas of librarianship. A career as public library reference librarian is at the top of my list. From your perspective as a senior manager with the Prince William Public Library System, I am very interested in learning more about reference librarian work. Also, I would be interested in your thoughts about careers in public libraries.

I would be very grateful if I could meet with you briefly to gain some insights into these issues. I will call you next week to see if you might be willing to do this.

Once you make a successful contact, take this opportunity seriously. Treat this as a "real" interview in terms of dress and how you present yourself. While there is no specific job for which you are being interviewed, you want to be remembered favorably should something arise in the future. Even if this individual doesn't have a job available, there is always the possibility that the employer will pass your name on to someone else. You don't want to put this person under any pressure, so this is not the time to ask for a job.

The informational interview is also an excellent opportunity to ask questions and explore areas of librarianship that you may want to pursue. Some questions you might consider include:

- What additional experience/education should I seek to pursue this area of librarianship?
- Which professional activities would you recommend pursuing?
- What are salaries like in this area of librarianship?
- Who else would you recommend that I speak to?

Also, be sure to take your resume with you and follow up with a thank-you letter.

> The informational interview is also an excellent opportunity to ask questions and explore areas of librarianship that you may want to pursue.

SCREENING

Many libraries use screening interviews to ascertain that you meet minimum qualifications. You often find that the selecting official is not part of this process. Rather, this task is frequently relegated to a human resource specialist or a lower-level staff member. The basic goal is to validate your application so you can be sent off to the next level. Clearing this step is vital to reaching the final interview stage, so be sure that you take this process very seriously and invest the same amount of time in preparation. Generally, screening interviews are done by telephone. The next section deals with tips for managing telephone interviews.

TELEPHONE

Telephone interviews are increasingly popular because libraries are unable to pay for travel expenses for potential job applicants. If you are very serious about the position and consider yourself a strong candidate, you might think about traveling at your own expense. Since that is often difficult, either because of expense or time away from work, a telephone interview will have to suffice.

Interviews by telephone are very tricky since there is no opportunity to observe facial expressions and body language. Conveying qualities such as enthusiasm are often very difficult to communicate by telephone. So it is especially important that you use your voice as much as possible to convey these qualities. Focus on diction, and keep your voice as animated as possible. Don't speak too rapidly—remember, the interviewers are taking notes.

Try not use a cell phone, since the sound quality and connection maybe problematic. Make sure you are in a quiet place with no distractions such as a crying baby, barking dog, or TV in the background. While the temptation might be to conduct the interview in your bathrobe and fuzzy slippers, it is probably advisable to get dressed so you are speaking and feeling the part of a professional. One big advantage is that you can have everything you need in front of you—resume, notes, etc.

Follow up with all the same steps, such as a thank-you note, that you would with an in-person interview.

ONE-ON-ONE VS. GROUP

Group or panel interviews are generally the most common type of interviews today. Developing a rapport with just one interviewer is far easier than a group. With a panel interview, however, make sure you engage every participant when you speak. This literally means making eye contact with all of the panelists. As described in the earlier section on greeting interviewers, make sure you shake hands at the beginning and end of the interview with each panelist. Also, make sure you get the correct pronunciation of their names.

MEAL-TIME

No other part of the interview is fraught with as much peril as having a meal with the interviewer. In lengthy interviews, especially in academic settings, taking the candidate to lunch is part of the drill. This is not the time to relax and unwind. This seemingly informal part of the interview is a critical part of the process. The interviewers will be most interested to see how you function in a social situation.

Avoid any types of messy food such as soup, spaghetti, or something that might be difficult to cut on your plate. Avoid garlic or foods with lingering odors. If your interviewer has an alcoholic beverage, it might be advisable to have one as well. Otherwise, don't consume alcoholic beverages.

A CRASH COURSE ON INTERVIEW TIPS

When you are faced with an interview and only have limited time to prepare, and there is no opportunity to review these chapters, here are some of the most critical interview survival tips:

- Bring copies of your current resume.
- Check out the location of the interview in advance so you know where to show up.
- Arrive at the interview location 10 minutes in advance.
- Dress conservatively.
- Shake hands firmly but avoid finger-crushing grips.
- Smile, be enthusiastic and display energy.
- Don't drone on and on; when you have answered a question, stop talking.
- Vary the tone of your voice; speak slowly and with confidence.
- Never criticize your current employer.
- Quantify your answers when possible.
- Always think in terms of results. What did you produce?
- Try to smile and look like you are enjoying the interview.
- Maintain good eye contact.
- Don't ask questions about salary or benefits.
- At the end of the interview, ask some questions about the position and the library.
- Always make a short closing statement summing up your qualifications.
- Thank the employer for the interview.

SOURCE A:
FILL YOUR RESUME
WITH ACTION VERBS

accelerated
accessioned
accomplished
achieved
acquired
acted
active in
adapted
added
addressed
adjusted
administered
advised
advocated
allocated
analyzed
applied
appointed
appraised
approved
arranged
articulated
assembled
assessed
assigned
assimilated
assisted
assumed
attained
audited
augmented
authorized
balanced
broadened
budgeted
built
cataloged
chaired
changed
clarified
classified

coached
collected
communicated
compared
compiled
completed
composed
coordinated
conceived
conducted
consolidated
constructed
consulted
contacted
contributed
controlled
converted
coordinated
corrected
corresponded
counseled
created
critiqued
decreased
defined
delegated
delivered
demonstrated
described
designated
designed
determined
developed
devised
directed
displayed
distributed
documented
doubled
drafted
earned

edited
educated
effected
eliminated
employed
enacted
encouraged
engaged
enlarged
enlisted
established
estimated
evaluated
examined
executed
exercised
exhibited
expanded
expedited
facilitated
finalized
followed up
forecasted
formed
formulated
fostered
founded
functioned
furnished
gathered
generated
guided
halved
handled
headed
helped
identified
illustrated
implemented
improved
improvised

increased	planned	sparked
influenced	pinpointed	spoke
informed	prepared	staffed
initiated	presented	standardized
innovated	processed	started
inspected	procured	stimulated
instituted	produced	stored
instructed	proficient	streamlined
integrated	programmed	strengthened
interpreted	promoted	stressed
interviewed	proposed	stretched
introduced	proved	structured
invented	provided	studied
investigated	published	submitted
involved	purchased	succeeded
issued	raised	suggested
justified	reallocated	summarized
launched	received	superseded
lead	recommended	supervised
learned	reconciled	supplied
lectured	recruited	supported
led	redesigned	surveyed
located	reduced	tailored
logged	referred	taught
made	regulated	terminated
maintained	reinforced	tested
managed	reported	traced
marketed	represented	tracked
measured	requested	traded
mediated	requisitioned	trained
modified	researched	transferred
molded	resolved	transformed
monitored	responsible for	translated
motivated	revamped	trimmed
negotiated	reviewed	tripled
notified	revised	turned
observed	scheduled	tutored
obtained	screened	uncovered
operated	searched	unified
ordered	secured	updated
organized	served	upgraded
oversaw	serviced	used
participated	set up	utilized
perceived	simplified	verified
performed	sold	won
persuaded	solved	wrote
pioneered		

GENERAL SUBJECT INDEX

JOB OBJECTIVES AND POSITION TITLE INDEX

WORK HISTORY INDEX

(To Locate a Particular Job for Ideas on Useful One-Liner Descriptions)

ABOUT THE AUTHOR

Robert R. Newlen is the Head of the Legislative Relations Office of the Congressional Research Service, Library of Congress, where he has worked for 30 years. He graduated with a B.A. from Bridgewater College, an M.A. from The American University, and an M.S.L.S. from The Catholic University. He is a frequent speaker on resume writing and interviewing. He has served as Director of the Board of the District of Columbia Library Association, a member of the Executive Board of the American Library Association, and as a Trustee of the American Library Association Endowment.